WHISPERINGS of the SPIRIT

WHISPERINGS *of the* SPIRIT

NANCY MURPHY

DESERET
BOOK

Salt Lake City, Utah

Library of Congress Cataloging-in-Publication Data

Murphy, Nancy, 1957-
   Whisperings of the spirit / Nancy Murphy.
     p. cm.
   ISBN-13: 978-1-59038-869-3 (hardbound : alk. paper)
  1. Holy Spirit.   2. Spiritual life—The Church of Jesus Christ of Latter-day Saints.   3. The Church of Jesus Christ of Latter-day Saints—Doctrines. I. Title.
   BX8643.H63M87 2008
   231'.3—dc22   2007046816

Printed in the United States of America
Worzalla Publishing Co., Stevens Point, WI

10   9   8   7   6   5   4   3   2   1

To my children and grandchildren
May you seek to hear the Spirit's whisperings
every day of your lives

CONTENTS

CONTENTS

ACKNOWLEDGMENTS

With many thanks and deep appreciation to my parents, Claude and Bonnie Thomas, for rearing me in a home where the Spirit was always present; to my husband, Dale, whose patient love has been an anchor in my life and whose ever-constant example has inspired me to seek the Spirit every day; and to my children and their spouses, who constantly amaze me with the goodness of their lives and their sensitivity to the still small voice.

INTRODUCTION

When the Lord blessed us with the Holy Ghost in mortality, he bestowed upon us one of his most tender mercies. As we recognize the whisperings of the Spirit in our own lives and act upon his guidance, we invite him to remain in our lives as our constant companion. Only with his gentle and wise instruction can we safely maneuver our way through mortality and return to our Father's presence. Because of this, our relationship with the Holy Ghost is not only important but crucial.

Come with me as we learn together how to hear, recognize, listen to, record, and live by the whisperings of the Spirit. At the end of each chapter you will find suggestions you may follow to deepen your relationship with the Holy Ghost. Each step will take you closer to him and lead you to the path where you may walk constantly by his side. As you spend a few minutes completing each small task, you will break down barriers, be more aware of his presence, and feel a renewed connection with the Holy Ghost. You will see him more readily in everyday experiences and more clearly be able to hear his voice. When that happens, you will have transformed these simple pages of information into a lasting and very personal experience as you truly live by the whisperings of the Spirit.

CHAPTER ONE

PERSONAL PROMPTINGS

And upon these I write the things of my soul.
2 NEPHI 4:15

No one ever wants to borrow my books. To be honest, they are a mess, filled as they are with an assortment of lines and colors, notes and turned-down corners as reminders of the things I have gleaned from their pages—things I just don't want to forget. Even though I am only an average reader who reads only an average number of books, I could never possibly remember everything I have read. There is simply too much to be retained. It seems to me that forgetting what you read is just the same as never reading at all, so I make a point to leave each book ready to remind me of the things it first taught me.

As I contemplate the workings of the Spirit in my life, I have come to realize that those pencil scrawls and faded colors represent the moments the Holy Ghost spoke to my heart, identifying things I specifically needed to know at a particular time in my life. The more familiar I become with the voice of the Spirit, the more easily I recognize the information—be it in a book or a talk in sacrament meeting—that is most applicable to me. Once identified, those are things I know I must remember.

In an effort to do that, I began a journal of sorts, a record of things that have touched my heart, taught me truths, and given me understanding of who I am and who the Lord would have me become. This journal is filled with everyday experiences that are common to us all and yet are often overlooked because we do not recognize the source from whence they spring and, thus, their spiritual significance. My journal is a priceless treasure in my life, a deep and revitalizing spiritual well that I draw from constantly. Just as the prophets of old recorded for their posterity the times the Spirit spoke to them, this journal—my "scripture journal"—is a record for my posterity of the times the Spirit has spoken to me. I want my children and grandchildren to know that the Lord knew me personally, as evidenced by the Holy Ghost giving me individual instruction and personal inspiration. And I want those I love to know that, because the Lord loves all of his children, they too can receive individual instruction—the Holy Ghost will speak to them as they seek him. Through my scripture journal, cherished lessons of a divine tutor can be remembered and applied long after I am gone.

Keeping a scripture journal has taught me to listen more carefully for the whisperings of the Spirit. This personal record has provided me with rich, spiritual experiences as it draws from both my heart and my mind communications from the Holy Ghost—many of which, until recently, I was completely unaware I was receiving. As I have written in my journal, I have felt the Spirit near. A friend who now keeps her own scripture journal told me, "I didn't know all those things I heard in my mind and felt in my heart were really the Holy Ghost speaking. Keeping a scripture journal has taught me how to pay better attention. Now that I finally know how to hear him, *I really listen.*"

The Holy Ghost enters every corner of our lives. As we look more closely, we find him everywhere. His voice is constant, if only we have ears to hear.

A few years ago I began to feel an intense yearning to know my grandparents who had lost their lives in a tragic accident a few years before I was born. I wanted anything that had belonged to them—even buttons from a shirt would do. Funny how something they had owned could fill such a hole in my life, but when you do not have the people you love, you will settle for anything. One day a package arrived from my uncle. Two small ceramic statues, made by my grandmother years before, lay inside the box. I cried for a week. Those fragile figurines now sit in a glass-fronted cabinet next to my bed, a constant reminder of grandparents I never knew. They are treasures in my life worth more to me than gold—not because of what they are but because of what they represent.

Much like my grandmother's precious figurines, the impressions that come to me through the Holy Ghost are treasures because of what they represent—the softly communicated love of my Father in Heaven. Because I cherish such heavenly impressions, I cannot hear them and then neglect them; I cannot listen and then simply brush them aside. I must write them down, learn from them, reflect on them, and continually strive to live by every single whisper.

Communicating with the Spirit is a process, not an event. As we grow in experience, we grow in understanding, for time and effort fine-tune our ability to recognize the Spirit's voice. He will prompt us. We must realize, remember, and record those things he declares on the Lord's behalf. The words in our scripture journals will be lasting reminders of testimonies gained through the quiet whisperings of the Spirit, the whisperings that should be making a profound difference in our lives.

Gratitude is the driving force behind the desire to record lessons learned through the Holy Ghost. Elder Richard G. Scott taught us how to express this gratitude: "Spiritually sensitive information should be kept in a sacred place that communicates to the Lord how you treasure it." And he gave another reason for recording these promptings: "That practice enhances the likelihood of your receiving further light" ("Acquiring," 88).

As we show the Lord how deeply we value what he gives, he

will give us more. Thus we establish a pattern of spiritual education throughout our entire lives.

STEP ONE

Begin with a blank book or journal. On the first page, write a letter to your children. Explain that this book is your "scripture journal" because it is a sacred record of the times the Spirit has spoken to you. Express your desire for them to know you better by reading this journal which is filled with accounts of the times when you were inspired by the Holy Ghost. Ask them to treasure the journal and pass it on to their children, so that your experiences may continue to bless those you love, despite the generations that separate you, for many, many years to come.

From the scripture journal of Mormon:

> *I do this for a wise purpose; for thus it whispereth me, according to the workings of the Spirit of the Lord which is in me.*
>
> —WORDS OF MORMON 1:7

From the scripture journal of Jacob:

> *The Lord God poured in his Spirit into my soul.*
>
> —JACOB 7:8

CHAPTER TWO

LIVE BY THE WHISPERINGS OF THE SPIRIT

If we live in the Spirit, let us also walk in the Spirit.
GALATIANS 5:25

An intriguing piece of art hangs on a wall in our home. At first glance, it appears to be completely blank—just a white piece of paper matted in a wooden frame. But as you walk closer and when the light is just right, you begin to see shadows and soft lines—intricately arranged in such a way as to direct your eye to the words they reveal: "Live by the Whisperings of the Spirit." Artist James H. Fedor is responsible for this beautiful, thought-provoking piece. He explained his purpose in its creation:

"Years ago, I had a dream in which I made an art piece painted only with light. This blind embossed print—*Whisperings*—is the realization of my dream. It is the closest symbolism I could imagine to the quiet impressions of the Spirit. I wanted a piece which would be almost invisible until and only when it was illuminated from a one-directional light source. This reminds me that some things, particularly those things of the Spirit, can only be seen in a certain light.

"I chose the whitest paper I could find as the other part of my art expression. Purity of soul is an inner condition enabling one to hear the still, small voice of the Spirit. This piece reminds me daily to study to be still, study to be pure. When the mind is still and pure it is prepared to receive the Spirit and hear the voice of God."

Several years ago, after my husband was called to preside over the Massachusetts Boston Mission, we took this print with us and hung it in a prominent spot in the mission home. When new missionaries arrived from the Missionary Training Center each month, we held a short testimony meeting in our living room. During these meetings, President Murphy would ask a missionary seated at the far end of the room to stand and read the words on the framed white print. With a look of dismay, the missionary would usually turn red and admit that he could not see anything at all on the paper. President Murphy would then ask him to come a few steps closer and give it another try. A look of relief always washed over the missionary's face when he was finally within range and could make out the previously invisible words, which he would then read aloud: "Live by the Whisperings of the Spirit." As the message of the print became clear, so did its underlying lesson:

We cannot *live* by the whisperings of the Spirit unless we

If we wish to hear the Spirit speak to us we must remove the distractions that keep us from hearing it.

9

are *close* to the Spirit. The closer we are to him, the more clearly we can feel his influence and hear his guiding voice.

The whisperings of the Spirit will become more familiar the more intently we seek to hear and understand them. Eventually they become as comfortable and soothing as the voice of a loved one or the companionship of an old friend. The more we recognize the language of the Spirit by which these promptings are communicated, and the more experience we have in listening to the Spirit's voice, the more consistently we will hear him. Perhaps this is one thing President Heber J. Grant had in mind when he said, "That which we persist in doing becomes easier for us to do; not that the nature of the thing itself is changed, but that our power to do is increased" (*Standards,* 353). Our ability to hear the Spirit's whisperings will greatly increase as we more consistently listen for them. It takes practice to develop spiritual ears and learn to hear with our hearts.

The biblical account of Naaman, a Syrian captain and a leper, teaches a valuable lesson. To cure his leprosy, Naaman was instructed by the prophet Elisha to bathe seven times in the River Jordan. At first Naaman refused, but eventually he followed the prophet's counsel and, after washing in the river, emerged completely free of his affliction. We may ask, Which of the seven baths actually cured him? The third one? The fifth? The sixth? Admittedly, to pose such questions is to miss the intended message, for the Lord's promise was only fulfilled when the *entire* requirement was completed—no one single moment brought about Naaman's miracle. It was obedience to the assignment *in its entirety* that made all the difference.

Similarly, gaining the ability to hear the Holy Ghost does not come in an instant or at the completion of any particular task. It is impossible to pinpoint the exact moment in which we become aware of the Spirit's presence and gain sensitivity to his words. It is the gradual accumulation of every whisper, every prompting, and every moment of inspiration that teaches us how to strengthen our lines of communication with him. For this reason, it takes sustained effort and gradual, consistent growth to become receptive to the voice of the Holy Ghost. With time, we can develop spiritual sensitivity like that of Michelangelo, who explained the insight he experienced as he created his sculpture *Angel with Candlestick:* "I saw the angel in the marble and carved until I set him free" (ThinkExist.com).

The companionship of the Holy Ghost is unmatched in its ability to profoundly affect the course of our lives. When heeded, the voice of the Holy Ghost can accomplish more in our lives than any other single influence. Its value cannot be measured. It is a treasure without equal, a pearl of great price. But guidance alone is not all he brings. As our constant companion, he also brings joy, contentment, and peace.

The Holy Ghost will not fail us, and his steady guidance is freely available to all who seek it in righteousness. His inspiration will always be correct; his gentle voice will always speak the truth. We need never question lessons taught, answers revealed, or inspiration given, for it is contrary to eternal law for him ever to lead us astray.

No other source of testimony can compare to the rock-solid foundation that is established when the Spirit speaks. President James E. Faust taught: "The Holy Ghost bears witness to us of the truth and impresses upon our souls the reality of God the Father and His Son, Jesus Christ, so surely that no earthly power or authority can separate us from that knowledge" ("Born," 58).

Another reason the Holy Ghost makes such a lasting impression is that he becomes a part of our being through our feelings, his primary vehicle of communication. A wise man once said, "They may forget what you say, but they will never forget the way you make them feel." As time passes, we may forget details of an experience, but the feelings within us will remain forever. We may struggle to recall the exact words of a particularly touching prayer or an inspiring fireside talk, but we will long remember the feelings it planted in the fertile soil of our hearts. The cluttered strings of facts and details are often difficult to recall, but the feelings of the soul are deeply rooted, forever cherished, and, therefore, always more easily remembered. The testimony given by the Holy Ghost is the most solid and secure witness we can receive. The scriptures are filled with examples of those who received visitations yet still were not truly converted, as well as accounts of those who, upon receiving a witness from the Holy Ghost, gained testimonies that were unshakable. We are reminded of Laman and Lemuel who stood in the presence of an angel yet still openly rebelled against God. President Joseph Fielding Smith explained, "The Spirit of God speaking to the spirit of man has power to impart truth with greater effect and understanding than the truth can be imparted by personal contact even with heavenly beings" (*Doctrines,* 1:47–48).

"What greater witness can you have than from God?" (D&C 6:23). Indeed, the Holy Ghost is the source of the most lasting manifestations of truth. Although he separated himself from the Church, Martin Harris's testimony of the Book of Mormon and the prophetic calling of the Prophet Joseph Smith could not be shaken. It was a testimony bestowed by the Holy Ghost—and it eventually led Martin Harris back to full fellowship with the Saints.

The Lord's purposes on earth could not be accomplished were it not for the Holy Ghost. As part of his divine mission, he guides and inspires mankind and, by so doing, brings to pass those things outlined by the Lord. The scriptures teach that the Lord's will is accomplished by the "pour[ing] out [his] Spirit upon all flesh" (D&C 95:4). In fact, Christopher Columbus is one who acknowledged the divine source of his inspiration: "Our Lord unlocked my mind, sent me upon the sea, and gave me fire for the deed. Those who heard of my emprise called it foolish, mocked me, and laughed. But who can doubt but that *the Holy Ghost inspired me?*" (Wasserman, *Columbus,* quoted in Petersen, *Prologue,* 26).

The Holy Ghost plays a critical role in the plan of salvation, for it is only through the Spirit that we can truly know the Savior and fully develop our relationship with him, two essential steps in our quest toward perfection. Were it not for the promptings of the Holy Ghost in this mortal realm, we could not fulfill a crucial requirement for exaltation: spiritual intimacy with our beloved Savior. Just as the Holy Ghost leads us to Christ, so it is *only* through the Spirit that we can truly come to know the Master. The Holy Ghost points us to all things celestial for, as Elder Neal A. Maxwell explained, "when we have the Spirit with us, it means we have achieved significant Christ-centeredness in our lives, for we cannot be close to one member of the Godhead without being close to all three" (*Notwithstanding,* 112).

All three members of the Godhead work in concert to lead us through mortality, as evidenced by their divided stewardships and combined influence on our lives. This holy triad works together with one purpose—the salvation and exaltation of God's children. We pray to our Father in Heaven, who created us, in the name of the Son, who redeemed us. The Holy Ghost testifies of them both and leads us along the path of righteousness, communicating with us spiritually to keep us safe and strong.

Many years ago, the Mutual Improvement Association adopted the slogan "We Stand for Divine Guidance" (Alldredge, *Era,* Dec. 1923, 114). It would be well for us to take into our hearts the same motto, to seek always for divine guidance, which comes to us through the still, small voice of the Holy Ghost. His is the voice that will help us, teach us, and lead us home to our Father in Heaven, who longs for our return. Because of his infinite love for us, he has given us a companion to walk by our side and illuminate the pathway to exaltation.

The Holy Ghost is always whispering to us. The only real question is, Are we listening?

STEP TWO

Practice listening for the Spirit's promptings in your life. Sometimes a prompting will come as an idea or a thought accompanied by a warm feeling. Promptings could even be described as "aha" moments—the catchphrase the world uses for a sudden recognition of truth. In your scripture journal, make a list of at least five ways the Spirit speaks to you. Pay close attention, listen intently, and record one prompting or bit of inspiration you hear each day this week. As you open your ears and make it a habit to listen for the Holy Ghost, you will hear him every single day of your life.

From the scripture journal of Joseph Smith:

> *Learn of me, and listen to my words; walk in the meekness of my Spirit.*
> —DOCTRINE AND COVENANTS 19:23

CHAPTER THREE

WHO IS THE HOLY GHOST?

The Holy Ghost . . . is a personage of Spirit.
DOCTRINE AND COVENANTS 130:22

Elder L. Lionel Kendrick once said, "In the economy of heaven the Lord never uses a floodlight when a flashlight is sufficient" (*Speeches*, 256). In other words, the Lord does not reveal volumes on a subject when one page will do. Because of his love for us, our Father in Heaven always reveals those things on which our salvation depends. He gives us what is necessary and essential. In this way, he establishes the divine dividing line between those things for which we will be held accountable and those for which we will not, for we are never responsible for knowledge we do not have. When we understand this principle, we realize that all the information he bestows on us has a predetermined purpose and that any piece of the divine puzzle that seems to be missing has been concealed by heavenly design.

Such is the case as we explore the question, Who is the Holy Ghost? There is much on this subject we do not know. There is, however, much we *do* know about the Holy Ghost, and we can assume it is sufficient. The critical issue is not that we have every answer and satisfy every curiosity but simply that we learn to hear his voice, seek his influence, and earn the right to his sanctifying presence in our lives. The specific details given us concerning him are limited to those that will help us accomplish this task.

As the third member of the Godhead, the Holy Ghost stands next to God the Father, Elohim, and God the Son, Jesus Christ. We know that the Holy Ghost does not possess a body of flesh and bones, as do both the Father and the Son. Modern revelation tells us: "The Father has a body of flesh and bones as tangible as man's; the Son also; but the Holy Ghost has not a body of flesh and bones, but is a personage of Spirit. Were it not so, the Holy Ghost could not dwell in us" (D&C 130:22). Because the Holy Ghost is a personage of spirit, we might assume his specific mission could not be accomplished with the restrictions of a mortal body. Because he is a God, we can be certain that he is perfect and carries with him all the rights, responsibilities, and powers of godhood.

What else do we know about the Holy Ghost? What other information is vital to our developing a relationship with him?

Elder James E. Talmage taught concerning His nature and

mortal mission: "The Holy Ghost undoubtedly possesses personal powers and affections; these attributes exist in Him in perfection. Thus, He teaches and guides, testifies of the Father and the Son, reproves for sin, speaks, commands, and commissions, makes intercession for sinners, is grieved, searches and investigates, entices, and knows all things. These are not figurative expressions, but plain statements of the attributes and characteristics of the Holy Ghost." He then gives us this insight concerning the personage of the Holy Ghost: "That the Spirit of the Lord is capable of manifesting Himself in the form and figure of man, is indicated by the wonderful interview between the Spirit and Nephi, in which He revealed Himself to the prophet, questioned him concerning his desires and belief, instructed him in the things of God, speaking face to face with the man. 'I spake unto him,' says Nephi, 'as a man speaketh; for I beheld that he was in the form of a man; yet nevertheless, I knew that it was the Spirit of the Lord; and he spake unto me as a man speaketh with another'" (*Articles*, 144–45).

A common misconception about the Holy Ghost concerns the form of his being as it relates to his presence at the baptism of Christ. Some interpret scripture to mean that the Holy Ghost was there that day in the form of a dove. Joseph Smith clarified, however, that the Holy Ghost "is in the form of a personage. [He] cannot be transformed into a dove; but the sign of a dove was given to John [the Baptist] to signify the truth of the deed, as the dove is an emblem or token of truth and innocence" (*Teachings*, 276).

The Holy Ghost is a personage, not merely an abstract thought or figurative idea. He exists as surely as you and I do. Because he has a spirit body, in contrast to a physical body, we sometimes forget he has a body at all. President Joseph Fielding Smith taught: "As a spirit personage the Holy Ghost has size and dimensions. He does not fill the immensity of space, and cannot be everywhere present in person at the same time" (*Doctrines*, 1:38).

It is the power of the Holy Ghost—not the personage—that can touch us all simultaneously and inspire many hearts at once. We do not know just how he accomplishes such a task, but therein lies the manifestation of his godhood.

We see evidence in the world today that Satan has distorted the important truth concerning the Spirit's ability to dwell within us and by so doing has created doubt concerning God himself. He has given credence to the thought that God the Father can dwell in many places and many hearts at once, feeding the mistaken idea that God exists without form and shares no similarity with man. With his usual methods of deception, Satan attempts to depersonalize God and cause confusion about His nature by suggesting that He is an abstract essence of some sort, an incomprehensible being that can be everywhere at once to fill the vast universe and yet dwell in a single heart. Making Him appear as unlike man as possible (no body), Satan has attempted to remove from us any inkling of our spiritual genealogy, hoping to convince us that we have never had and never could have a personal relationship with God. Unfortunately,

19

many in the world believe Satan's lie and, as a result, forfeit the opportunity to know their Father in Heaven. They have forgotten him. Blind to the blessings of their divine parentage and the importance of that heavenly parent-mortal child relationship, many wander through life completely unaware of what they have given up.

As planned in premortal councils, the Savior came to earth with a divine mission essential to the plan of salvation. Similarly, the Holy Ghost, sharing in the responsibilities of the Godhead, has also been set apart to fulfill a foreordained mission. To more fully understand what that mission entails, we need only look at the ways he manifests himself in our lives. "He is the Comforter," Elder Bruce R. McConkie explained. "Testator, Revelator, Sanctifier, Holy Spirit, Holy Spirit of Promise, Spirit of Truth, Spirit of the Lord, and Messenger of the Father and the Son and his companionship is the greatest gift that mortal man can enjoy. His mission is to perform all of the functions appertaining to the various name-titles which he bears" (*Mormon Doctrine*, 359). President Brigham Young called him "the special gift of the Father" (*Discourses*, 160). Through the Spirit, the thoughts and desires of the Father and the Son are made known to us, and we are taught things we can know in no other way.

Communication from God also comes to us as the Spirit inspires others to speak. President Wilford Woodruff taught, "When a man speaks as he is moved upon by the Holy Ghost, it is the spirit of inspiration; it is the word of God; it is the will of God" (*Discourses,* 5). Alma received inspiration from the Lord through the Holy Ghost and called his people to repentance, asking them if they had "experienced this mighty change in [their] hearts" (Alma 5:14).

In one of the most beautiful and profound sermons ever recorded, Alma then explained the source of his knowledge and testimony:

"And this is not all. Do ye not suppose that I know of these things myself? Behold, I testify unto you that I do know that these things whereof I have spoken are true. And how do ye suppose that I know of their surety?

"Behold, I say unto you they are made known unto me by the Holy Spirit of God. Behold, I have fasted and prayed many days that I might know these things of myself. And now I do know of myself that they are true; for the Lord God hath made them manifest unto me by his Holy Spirit" (Alma 5:45–46).

Those of Alma's people who had ears to hear certainly received a witness that day. Bearing witness is another function of the Holy Ghost. If we have a testimony of God the Father and Jesus Christ, it is because the Holy Ghost has borne witness to us of them. That testimony will not only lead us to the narrow path spoken of by Nephi (2 Nephi 31:18) but will keep us on it, if we remain righteous and keep our ears open to the Spirit's guiding voice.

Elder James E. Talmage described additional responsibilities of the Spirit: "The Holy Ghost may be regarded as the minister of the Godhead, carrying into effect the decisions of the

Supreme Council" (*Articles*, 145). That is why the Spirit, acting as an agent (or minister) of the Godhead, can speak to our hearts and minds on behalf of the Father and the Son. He is their representative, their emissary, their delegate, their ambassador, their mouthpiece. The only way we receive communication from them—other than through personal visitations—is through the Holy Ghost. Doctrine and Covenants 97:1 confirms, "I speak unto you with [the] voice . . . of my Spirit." Knowing this, we can easily see how, without the third member of the Godhead, we would be utterly lost—unable to progress and incapable of spiritual growth. Left alone, cut off from any communication with our Father in Heaven, we would live out our time in mortality robbed of purpose and the chance to progress.

President Joseph Fielding Smith explained that the Holy Ghost also "has the mission to teach those who keep the covenants they make with the Lord" (*Answers*, 2:146). Being true to our covenants puts us in a position to receive the voice of the Lord through the Holy Ghost, "for mine elect hear my voice and harden not their hearts" (D&C 29:7). Honoring covenants opens the door to the Spirit's constant instruction.

Fresh from the waters of baptism, we first become acquainted with the Holy Ghost as we are given, by the laying on of hands, the privilege of his companionship. It is then and through him that our sins are remitted. Nephi taught, "For the gate by which ye should enter is repentance and baptism by water; and then cometh a remission of your sins by fire and by the Holy Ghost" (2 Nephi 31:17). It is he who brings about the purifying change in us. Elder Bruce R. McConkie explained: "Sins are remitted not in the waters of baptism, as we say in speaking figuratively, but when we receive the Holy Ghost. It is the Holy Spirit of God that erases carnality and brings us into a state of righteousness. We become clean when we actually receive the fellowship and companionship of the Holy Ghost" (*Witness*, 290).

Once our sins are forgiven, the Holy Ghost makes it possible to for us to change, to become "new creatures" (Mosiah 27:26). Elder Orson Pratt taught: "Without the aid of the Holy Ghost, a person . . . would have but very little power to change his mind, at once, from its habituated course, and to walk in newness of life. Though his sins may have been cleansed away, yet so great is the force of habit, that he would, without being renewed by the Holy Ghost, be easily overcome, and contaminated by sin. Hence, it is infinitely important that the affections and desires should be, in a measure, changed and renewed, so as to cause him to hate that which he before loved, and to love that which he before hated: to thus renew the mind of man is the work of the Holy Ghost" (*Holy Spirit*, quoted in Millet, *Writings*, 519–20).

After guiding us through the process of repentance and causing our hearts to change, the Holy Ghost directs us along the path we then must follow. "For behold," continues Nephi, "if ye will enter in by the way, and receive the Holy Ghost, it will show unto you all things what ye should do" (2 Nephi

32:5). No matter what it may bring, we need never fear the future if the Holy Ghost is near us.

When we stepped through the veil into mortality, we were separated from our Father in Heaven. Knowing what was ahead, we must have felt great anticipation for the blessing of this life and our long-awaited opportunity to progress. But knowing what we were leaving behind, we surely felt deep sadness and even some anxiety as well. On the day we received the gift of the Holy Ghost in mortality, our spirits certainly rejoiced, for the distance between us and our Father in Heaven narrowed as the veil became thin. For when the Holy Ghost is operational in our lives, we are as close to the Lord as a mortal can be without standing in His presence. The manifestations of the Holy Ghost are like the gentle flow of a river, continually running and persistently reminding us of a loving Father in Heaven. For as long as we live on this earth, the Holy Ghost is our most sure connection to all dimensions of our heavenly home.

The apostle John taught that the Holy Ghost teaches us all things and brings all things to our remembrance (John 14:26). He shows us things to come (John 16:13) and guides us to truth (John 16:13). Without him, we cannot teach others, for learning does not become true knowledge until the witness of the Spirit is received. He cleanses and sanctifies the righteous (3 Nephi 27:19–22). He directs our path and leads us to salvation as he testifies of Christ: "When the Comforter is come, whom I will send unto you from the Father, even the Spirit of truth, which proceedeth from the Father, he shall testify of me"

(John 15:26). The Holy Ghost gives life to our relationship with the Savior, providing the way whereby we may know him: "No man can say that Jesus is the Lord, but by the Holy Ghost" (1 Corinthians 12:3).

It is through the Holy Ghost that we receive testimonies. President Joseph F. Smith spoke of his experience with the Spirit: "The Lord withheld marvels from me, and showed me the truth, line upon line, precept upon precept, here a little and there a little, until he made me to know the truth from the crown of my head to the soles of my feet, and until doubt and fear had been absolutely purged from me. He did not have to send an angel from the heavens to do this, nor did he have to speak with the trump of an archangel. By the whisperings of the still small voice of the Spirit of the living God, he gave to me the testimony I possess" (*Doctrine,* 7).

The wisdom of the Spirit supersedes all sources of wisdom we have ever known or ever will know. The Holy Ghost directs us to truth, as Jacob, the brother of Nephi, taught: "The Spirit speaketh the truth and lieth not. Wherefore, it speaketh of things as they really are, and of things as they really will be" (Jacob 4:13).

As missionaries are sent around the world to share the gospel message, they do not go to convince or to coerce. They go to teach the elect how to gain personal testimonies of the gospel of Jesus Christ for themselves. Like the Prophet Joseph Smith, who followed the admonition of James, any who lack wisdom can find answers by asking God (James 1:5). Through the Holy

Ghost, we can know the truth of all things (Moroni 10:5). We have the promises of prophets that anyone who seeks shall find.

The scriptural account of Enoch tells of his celestial city and the saints who dwelt therein—their righteousness, their sanctification, and their ultimate reward. Because "they were of one heart and one mind, and dwelt in righteousness," they were "taken up into heaven" (Moses 7:18, 21). But the story does not end there. We go on to read:

"And after that Zion was taken up into heaven, Enoch beheld, and lo, all the nations of the earth were before him;

" . . . and behold, the power of Satan was upon all the face of the earth.

"And he saw angels descending out of heaven; and he heard a loud voice saying: Wo, wo be unto the inhabitants of the earth.

"And he beheld Satan; and he had a great chain in his hand, and it veiled the whole face of the earth with darkness; and he looked up and laughed, and his angels rejoiced.

"And Enoch beheld angels descending out of heaven, bearing testimony of the Father and Son; and the Holy Ghost fell on many, and they were caught up by the powers of heaven into Zion" (Moses 7:23–27).

In these verses we see the powerful converting influence of the Holy Ghost. Generations of those who remained after the city of Enoch was translated—who had rejected prophets, turned away from righteousness, and deliberately embraced sin—were not a lost cause, after all. Despite the evil-saturated environment surrounding them in a world where Satan reigned, the Holy Ghost found many of them, fell upon them, testified to them, converted them, and brought them into the presence of God (Moses 7:27). Although the situation looked bleak, the influence of the Holy Ghost shone through the darkness, and many were spiritually saved.

After we gain a testimony, it is the Holy Ghost that gives it utterance. Because of his inspiration, we can bear witness to others: "And it shall come to pass, that if you shall ask the Father in my name, in faith believing, you shall receive the Holy Ghost, which giveth utterance, that you may stand as a witness of the things of which you shall both hear and see, and also that you may declare repentance unto this generation" (D&C 14:8).

When my husband presided over the Massachusetts Boston Mission, we quickly learned that the best way to motivate missionaries was to convert and strengthen *them*. Once they felt the Spirit speak to their own hearts, their personal testimonies provided all the encouragement they needed to work hard and give themselves to the Lord. The Holy Ghost gave expression to their testimonies and courage to open their mouths. As Elder M. Russell Ballard explained, "When we are truly converted, we cannot be restrained from testifying" ("Testimony," 41). Once we feel the witness of the Spirit, it naturally follows that we desire others to feel it as well.

The Holy Ghost gives us power. This power comes from God and the fulfillment of promises he has made to his children. The Prophet Joseph Smith said, "You shall begin to feel the whisperings of the Spirit of God . . . and you shall be endowed with power from on high" (*History,* 2:182). Such power always makes us more than we were before. In this way, the Holy Ghost expands our abilities and strengthens our capabilities. He shows us who we are as children of God and magnifies our inherited attributes. Elder John A. Widtsoe said, "When the servants of the Lord display a spiritual power beyond the command of man; when the grief-laden heart beats with joy; when failure is converted into victory, it is by the visitation of the Holy Ghost" (*Man,* 150).

The Holy Ghost is given as a comforter; he attends us in our grief, consoles us during times of disappointment, and encourages us through moments of despair. We all have observed his labors of love, either in our own lives or in the lives of others as they have passed through trials. Several missionaries who were with us in Boston lost close family members during the time they were serving. I remember one of them in particular. His brother, who had recently returned from his own mission, was killed in an automobile accident. My heart was devastated as I saw this young elder's pain and anguish upon receiving the news. I wondered how—or if—he could continue as a missionary. His grief was so profound and his loss so great. I thought of him constantly in the weeks that followed and called him occasionally to see how he was doing. A month after the accident, I saw him at zone conference. Expecting to see sorrow in his eyes, I was surprised to see light. Thinking I would find his countenance fallen and his heart full of despair, I found instead a young man radiant with joy and shining with the peace that only the gospel of Jesus Christ can bring. The Comforter had come. As this elder gave his heart and soul to the work, he was continually filled with the Spirit. And as the Spirit filled him, he began to heal, bit by bit and day by day. My own testimony grew by leaps and bounds that autumn day in Springfield, Massachusetts. Never since have I doubted the comforting and healing power of the Holy Ghost.

As we learn to listen and respond, the Holy Ghost inspires us with daily promptings. He walks with us when invited and speaks often, if we are sensitive to his voice. Through the Holy Ghost, we can be inspired with day-to-day direction, tailored to our individual lives.

Often, the Spirit will instruct us to do things we otherwise might not have done. As a matter of fact, it is possible that he may inspire us to take a path directly opposite that which our mortal minds tell us or that our own thinking suggests. It is in those moments that it is especially critical to listen, for we otherwise may find ourselves traveling the wrong direction, making decisions that put us out of step with our Father in Heaven, and working against his plan for our lives.

No experience equals that of witnessing the process by which the Holy Ghost touches hearts. As they carry the Spirit with them, full-time missionaries are privileged to observe this process often, and once they are witness to its power, they are forever changed. The rest of us catch a glimpse now and then of the Spirit's transforming influence in our own lives, as well as in the lives of those around us, and when those moments come, we in "stand all amazed" (*Hymns,* no. 193). Once we see the Spirit at work, we do not forget it. Once we feel his influence, we are never the same again.

As we begin to realize the many ways the Holy Ghost operates in our lives, we more fully understand the great magnitude of his calling. As we pay attention to his whisperings, we become aware of the myriad of ways he reveals himself to us and the countless times he demonstrates his power. As we walk with the Spirit, every day brings us closer to our Father in Heaven. There is no gift more valuable, no friend more needed, no blessing more essential than that of the Holy Ghost. The mission of the Savior is to bridge the way between mortality and everlasting life. The mission of the Holy Ghost is to direct us, step by step, across that bridge to exaltation. Both the Savior and the Holy Ghost share one purpose with the Father, and that is to save us.

STEP THREE

Spend a few minutes thinking about the many ways the Holy Ghost touches your life. Think of specific times when you have felt him in the following three ways: as he comforted you, as he testified to you, and as he inspired you. Record these in your scripture journal.

From the scripture journal of Joseph Smith:

And you shall have the Holy Ghost, which manifesteth all things which are expedient unto the children of men.

—DOCTRINE AND COVENANTS 18:18

The Holy Ghost shall be thy constant companion.

—DOCTRINE AND COVENANTS 121:46

From the scripture journal of Moroni:

. . . the Holy Ghost, which Comforter filleth with hope and perfect love.

—MORONI 8:26

CHAPTER FOUR

WE NEED HIM

And ye shall receive the Holy Ghost,
that ye may have all things made manifest.
MOSES 8:24

Teddy Roosevelt and his Rough Riders invaded Cuba during the Spanish-American War. The seas were rough and threatening as the men sailed near the coast in preparation for what would be known as the Battle of San Juan Hill. The dangerous waters prevented them from anchoring close to the beach, and the lifeboats were their only option. Before climbing into the boats, however, the men pushed the horses and mules overboard, hoping they would instinctively swim toward land. Some of the animals made it. Some, disoriented and afraid, drowned. Others, including Teddy Roosevelt's horse, Texas, became confused in the high, churning waves, lost their sense of direction, and began swimming out to sea. The men, tossed to and fro on the sea, were powerless to save their animals from certain death.

Suddenly, from the distant shore, came a piercing sound. A bugler, aware of the seemingly hopeless situation, had lifted his bugle and begun to play. He played loud and long, hoping to attract the attention of the ill-fated animals. Recognizing the familiar sound of the bugle and knowing to follow it, many turned and, with all their might, swam toward the clarion call. The sound of the bugle brought them safely to shore that day. In the confusion, it was the only clear sound they could hear. One single bugle—calling them to safety.

We, too, fight a battle every single day. Ever since Satan's premortal defeat, he has waged war on the children of God. Humiliated by truth, he immediately set his sights on those who followed Christ. Moses recounts that defining moment in the heavenly councils: "And he became Satan, yea, even the devil, the father of all lies, to deceive and to blind men, and to lead them captive at his will" (Moses 4:4). Still angry and determined to win, he assaults us from every side, attempting to bind us with chains and lead us into captivity. In the chaos and confusion of life, he hopes we will lose our sense of direction and move away from safety toward spiritual death. And then comes the rescuing call. The Holy Ghost—on constant watch—recognizes the danger and sounds the alarm. If we are worthy and aware, we recognize the warning. Hearing his familiar voice, we are led to safety. If not for his inspiring call, our situation would be hopeless.

We all need the Holy Ghost. Without him we would be unable to receive personal revelation or pray to a personal God for inspiration suited to our specific needs, believing we would receive it. We would be left to ourselves and would struggle to find our way. Through the Holy Ghost the realization of the promise of Moroni—the promise that we all can know truth for ourselves through the Spirit's voice—is made possible. Moroni instructs us to "ask God, the Eternal Father, in the name of Christ, if these things are not true; and if ye shall ask with a sincere heart, with real intent, having faith in Christ, he will manifest the truth of it unto you, by the power of the Holy Ghost. And by the power of the Holy Ghost ye may know the truth of all things" (Moroni 10:4–5).

Without the inspiration of the Holy Ghost, it would be impossible to return to our Father in Heaven. Elder Joseph F. Smith taught, "Without the aid of the Holy Spirit no mortal can walk in the straight and narrow way, being unable to discern right from wrong, the genuine from the counterfeit, so nearly alike can they be made to appear" (*Journal of Discourses,* 18:275). We could not make righteous choices and decisions, except by chance. We could never identify truth, never understand it, and certainly never live by it. Repentance, forgiveness, and sanctification would be impossible to achieve, as these are all functions of the Spirit. The same number of ways the Spirit operates in our lives is the same number of reasons we could not return to our Father in Heaven without his guidance. We need him, and we could not make it without him.

A loving Father in Heaven has given us this divine guide, knowing we simply do not have the ability to return home to him without assistance. Elder B. H. Roberts taught: "Mankind stand in some need of a strength superior to any they possess of themselves, to accomplish this work of rendering pure our fallen nature. Such strength, such power, such a sanctifying grace is conferred on man in being born of the Spirit—in receiving the Holy Ghost" (*Relationship,* quoted in Millet, *Writings,* 204). Our Father in Heaven would never leave us on our own, expecting us to achieve something so far beyond our reach. He knew we would need the help of the Holy Ghost if ever we were to return to be with Him again.

Likewise, without the Holy Ghost, this living, breathing church would die of spiritual starvation. Think of it. Prophets without revelation? That simply could never be. President Joseph Fielding Smith taught: "The fact is all the prophets had the Holy Ghost. They were led and directed by him. And without this power they would not have been prophets" (*Doctrines,* 3:46). The Holy Ghost has guided prophets throughout time and always will.

If it were not for the Holy Ghost, the priesthood would cease to be. The authority to act in God's name would be meaningless, because no priesthood holder could discern the will of God. The power of the priesthood would not exist, for the power of God is communicated through the Holy Ghost. Elder Charles A. Callis commented on the critical role the Spirit plays in the operation of the priesthood: "The Holy Ghost is the genius of the Holy Priesthood. Remove from this body of men, clothed with this power, dispossess them, if that were possible, of the guiding influence of the spirit of revelation and they would be as unproductive in the ministry as the dry sand on the seashore" (Conference Report, Apr. 1938, 100).

Only through the Holy Ghost can the priesthood function properly. Because revelation is the foundation of Christ's church and the Holy Ghost is key to the revelatory process, neither the priesthood nor the Church would survive without him.

The Holy Ghost is the facilitator of revelation in our individual lives as well. He is the messenger; only through him is spiritual communication possible. Elder Delbert L. Stapley stated:

"Without the Holy Ghost, one lives in spiritual darkness, blind to truth, unbelieving of heart, and apostate in feelings and teachings. . . .

"Revelation is God's plan of instructing his people and guiding his work and kingdom upon earth. The Holy Ghost, as a personage of spirit, has the power and capacity of touching the spirit of man (spirit to spirit) and influencing him for good and righteousness if he is tuned to its spiritual wave length. The Holy Ghost has the power to quicken one's mind and increase one's understanding and comprehension of divine and temporal things. Without it there can be no faith, hope, nor personal assurance of eternal life" (Conference Report, Oct. 1966, 113–14).

Our dependence on the Holy Ghost has always been part

of the plan, established eons ago. The veil, by necessity, is one of forgetfulness, making it essential that we rely on the spiritual insight available to us only as we use the gift of the Holy Ghost. We must put off the natural man—the part of us that might attempt to live without the Spirit—for we will never reach our eternal goals by relying solely on our own abilities. Those who try to do so will someday realize their error and regret it. President Spencer W. Kimball warned: "The Lord will not force himself upon people, and if they do not believe, they will receive no revelation. If they are content to depend upon their own limited calculations and interpretations, then, of course, the Lord will leave them to their chosen fate" ("Revelation," 77).

In his wisdom, the Lord created a plan that required us to depend on those with the ability to exalt us. Certain things are essential to our salvation, which we simply cannot do for ourselves. Only the Holy Ghost can guide us to the exaltation that only the Savior, through his atoning sacrifice, can provide.

Every step toward sanctification can only be taken as we walk side by side with the Holy Ghost. Knowing this, we would never undertake the challenge of mortality without him, for then all our efforts would be in vain. We must not take one step alone. Whether we intentionally turn away or simply distance ourselves from him through neglect matters little; the outcome is the same.

Living without the Holy Ghost is spiritual suicide. Without the Holy Ghost our efforts become frustrated, our journey toward exaltation bogged down in questions with no answers, indecision with no direction, and spiritual sickness that has no remedy. President James E. Faust taught, "Indeed, not having the gift of the Holy Ghost is somewhat like having a body without an immune system" ("Born," 58). Without the Spirit, we will never be what God intends us to be. We will always be less than our foreordained potential.

As we journey through a world filled with moral decay, where deadly hazards look innocent and mists of darkness often cloud our view, truly our only hope for safe passage is the guidance offered us by the Holy Ghost. Ever wise and sensitive to our needs, the Lord knew that we, like Lehi, would need a reliable compass to point the way.

Through the Holy Ghost, we receive guidance that can be acquired in no other way, for he is an indispensable element of our spiritual progression. All knowledge is gained and all truth identified through him. Only as we heed his promptings and follow the course he outlines will we ever achieve the spiritual standing necessary to qualify for exaltation. This heavenly friend, if we let him, will lead us back home.

The direction of the Holy Ghost is as critical to the nourishment of our spirits as food is to our physical bodies. From a spiritual standpoint, we need the Holy Ghost even more than we need air. Our bodies will one day die, but our spirits and their attributes will continue on eternally. Should not the development of our spirits—our spiritual strength—be more important than anything else? The Prophet Joseph Smith said, "Salvation cannot come without revelation" (*History,* 3:389). We know revelation cannot come without the Holy Ghost, so we see that without the Holy Ghost salvation is out of our reach and impossible to achieve.

Elder Boyd K. Packer said, "We all have the right to inspiration and direction by the Spirit of the Holy Ghost . . . we all live far below our privileges" ("Sure Way"). How could we fail to claim the blessings to which we are entitled? Knowing the value of the lost prize, how could we allow earthly distractions to divert us from its pursuit? How could we permit less important things to steal away our energy and focus? Is it possible that we have been given a gift whose true value we do not completely realize or fully appreciate?

Parents, in partnership with God, have been given great responsibility in regard to their children. The Lord has been plain: We must teach our children the gospel. Keeping them safe, spiritually as well as physically, is our ultimate goal. We must equip them with every possible means of defense as they face the well-planned attacks of an adversary whose great desire is their complete spiritual destruction. No parent would recommend to a child that he drive recklessly in the wrong direction down a crowded freeway. To even suggest such a thing is completely ridiculous. We would simply never do that! Yet, in a different way, we often fail to keep our children safe. We fail to alert them to the spiritual dangers around them that are sometimes less obvious but ultimately even more destructive, for the effects of spiritual dangers are eternal. We actually endanger our children spiritually when we do not teach them how to hear and respond to the promptings of the Holy Ghost. Such action is tantamount to seeing them in a burning building and failing to point out the fire escape. The Holy Ghost is their source of answers and solutions but, most important, rescue. Elder M. Russell Ballard gave us this analogy:

"The gift of the Holy Ghost intensifies our relationship with that member of the Godhead. In a way, it's like living next door to the fire house. Although everyone is entitled to fire department services, the safest person in town is the one who lives next door to the fire station. And that's what the gift of the Holy Ghost does—it makes him a part of our lives. It introduces the third member of the Godhead into our hearts and souls and puts him on duty in our lives—a tremendous advantage, to be sure, but only as long as we're willing to pay attention to his whisperings and promptings" (*Search*, 91–92).

Have we instilled in our children's hearts a longing for the Spirit in their lives? Have we fortified their defenses by teaching them how to listen for, recognize, and act upon his whisperings every single day? Do we direct them toward the light he casts upon their paths? We must do more than simply introduce our children to the Holy Ghost. We must help them develop a deep and lasting relationship with him. Nothing we can do for them is of greater significance and value than to teach them to walk in his light.

Knowing the tragic consequences of temptation and sin, we simply cannot allow our children to live below *their* privileges. We cannot always be with them to protect them, but the Holy

Ghost can. Dressing them in the armor of God will bring us comfort—and them safety—in the heat of the battle. We must give them the strength to stand against evil; the Holy Ghost will then show them how. We must equip them with ears to hear his voice; the Holy Ghost will then lead them gently along.

Before we left our heavenly home, did we ever think it possible that we would come to earth and *not* listen to the voice of the Holy Ghost? Would we have been surprised to know that we might *not* understand his promptings? That we might *not* listen carefully to his whisperings? It was clear to us then that the companionship of the Spirit would be crucial to us now as we walk the path of this mortal experience. It was a fact to which there would be no exceptions—we would all need his guidance if we ever hoped to return to our Father's presence.

When we entered mortality, forgetfulness fell upon us, and the memory of our life then—and the truths that we once knew—have faded away. They lie deep within our souls, waiting to be remembered and recalled in this mortal world through the inspiration of the Holy Ghost.

Think of it another way. If you were to give a party, yet sent no invitations, would you be surprised if no one came? If a friend stopped to see you and you told him you were too busy for company, would it surprise you if he left?

Our relationship with the Holy Ghost depends on our invitation, our welcoming hand, and the price we are willing to pay. Although his companionship is a gift, his influence is not free. We must earn the privilege; we must be worthy of this divine prize. Elder Bruce R. McConkie said it well: "There is no price too high . . . no struggle too severe, no sacrifice too great, if out of it all we receive and enjoy the gift of the Holy Ghost" (*Witness*, 253).

Our relationship with the Holy Ghost is one of the most significant of our lives, one that must be fostered and nurtured and never ignored. Living by the Spirit not only sets us apart from the rest of the world but it also identifies us as true disciples of Christ. As we make him our constant companion, we experience a refining process—one that cleanses, purifies, and sanctifies our lives. In the end, it is these very things that qualify us as belonging to the Lord.

Like the gentle and persistent beam of a lighthouse on a fog-ridden shore or the crisp sound of a distant bugle calling hearers to safety, the Holy Ghost will help us find our way. Every traveler in this mortal realm is dependent upon his guidance. Without him, we have no guarantee of safe passage, but with him, we will never lose our way.

STEP FOUR

Look in the Topical Guide of your copy of the Bible under "Holy Ghost, Mission of." Skim through the list of scriptures and identify at least five things the Spirit does for you. Record these in your scripture journal.

Next, identify something in your life—an attitude, a weakness, a habit, or an action—that may be keeping the Spirit from you, even in a small degree, and resolve to give it up. This will strengthen your relationship with the Holy Ghost and bring him into your life in a deeper and more meaningful way. Surely nothing you will give up could be worth more to you than that!

From the scripture journal of Nephi:

The Holy Ghost . . . will show unto you all things what ye should do.

—2 NEPHI 32:5

From the scripture journal of King Benjamin:

He has poured out his Spirit upon you, and has caused that your hearts should be filled with joy.

—MOSIAH 4:20

CHAPTER FIVE

WE CAN HEAR HIM

He that hath an ear, let him hear what the Spirit saith.
REVELATION 2:7

A friend of mine spent several weeks one summer helping to build a school in a small village in Africa. Every day, hundreds of children flocked around to watch the progress, their eyes hopeful for even the smallest morsel of food. Most of them were orphans; all of them were starving. Hunger was simply a way of life for them, a fact they lived—and died—with.

Looking out across the seemingly endless sea of children, a woman in the group spotted a young child who was almost lifeless. She noticed an older child holding his hand. When he let go, the younger boy was so weak that his arm fell limp to his side. She imagined him to be two or three years old but later discovered he was actually ten. Lifting him in her arms, she carried him to their bus, where she tried to give him food and water, hoping in some miraculous way to spare him from what seemed to be the inevitable. She turned to the priesthood holders in their group and asked them to give him a blessing. After locating some consecrated oil, they laid their hands on his head and prepared to bless the dying boy. Realizing they did not know his name, they addressed him in the way the Lord would certainly know him and the only way they did. They said, simply, "Child of God."

More important than our names or any other identifying characteristic is our divine heritage. We are *all* children of God. And because we are his children, he has given us the privilege of constant communication with him. As part of that royal birthright, he has given us the gift of the Holy Ghost. President Gordon B. Hinckley promised: "We know also that with the blessing of the Almighty, if we are true and faithful, if we listen to the whisperings of the Spirit and follow those whisperings, we can, with our brethren and sisters, bring miracles to pass and accomplish the purposes for which we have been called under a divinely given call" ("Helm," 59).

I have lived many years now listening for the whisperings of the Spirit in my life. There have been times when I have heard them more distinctly than others, and times when I have not heard them at all, not because the Spirit wasn't speaking to me but simply because I didn't always know how to recognize his voice.

The truth is the Holy Ghost speaks to us constantly. His

voice is ever-present, his influence always near. Elder Gene R. Cook taught: "If we are going to practice the truths we already know, we must be more careful to listen to the promptings of the Spirit. I am convinced that we receive many promptings for every one or two that we obey. We do not obey the promptings because we sometimes do not know that we are being prompted or because we think the promptings are from some other source within ourselves. I have learned in my limited experience that as we grow and become more spiritually mature, we will find that there are more and more promptings to help guide us to perform according to that which we already know" (*Living,* 77–78).

As we become more spiritually alert, we realize just how often the Holy Ghost inspires, prompts, teaches, and guides us. The help he offers is steady and consistent, a rhythm as constant as the rising and setting of the sun. Our challenge is to hear, recognize, understand, value, and then live by his promptings when they come. Only then can we truly claim the Holy Ghost as our constant companion.

Because he is the perfect author of a perfect plan, our Father in Heaven knew our progression in mortality would depend on our ability to communicate with him. Were that not possible, we would stumble aimlessly through life, kept from the realization of our own eternal possibilities. We would be "wandering stars" (Jude 1:13) in a sky full of heavenly wonders. From a spiritual perspective, we are merely infants, critically dependent on our Father's wisdom. He is a loving parent, who has provided ways for us to hear him as he instructs, corrects, and inspires us. He has provided the means whereby he can express feelings to us as he encircles us "in the arms of [his] love" (D&C 6:20).

Despite the distance between us, we need never feel alone. Through prayer, we speak to him. Through the whisperings of the Spirit, he speaks to us. These two things—prayer and the promptings of the Spirit—are intricately connected, as we are taught by Elder Gene R. Cook: "The Spirit speaks in a still, small voice, and we have to really listen and expect to be able to hear it or we will not be able to. If we would like to increase our ability to hear the voice, we may best accomplish that by learning how to pray without ceasing. The more we learn to pray throughout the day, in my experience, the more the promptings will come to inspire us about what to do" (*Raising*, 95).

The Lord reminded Joseph Smith and Oliver Cowdery that as often as they had asked, they had received instruction through the Holy Ghost (D&C 6:14). We are given the same promise and allowed the same privilege: Whenever we ask, the Lord will answer.

As baptized and confirmed members of The Church of Jesus Christ of Latter-day Saints, we have been given the gift of the Holy Ghost. This gift entitles us to his companionship, according to our faithfulness. Righteousness refines our spirits and prepares us to heed the Spirit's guidance. Personal righteousness qualifies us to receive the influence of the Holy Ghost in our lives. The scriptures teach that the obedient will receive the Holy Ghost, "whom God hath given to them that obey him" (Acts 5:32). To honor the Holy Ghost and what he does, we must pay the requisite price in righteousness. If we are not willing to pay that price by giving up our sins and walking the path outlined by our Father in Heaven, we will not feel the full effects of the Spirit's influence. Mosiah's counsel is directed to each of us: "Keep his commandments, that he may pour out his Spirit more abundantly upon you" (Mosiah 18:10).

When the static of sin jams our spiritual airwaves, we cannot hear the promptings of the Holy Ghost nor are we deserving of his holy guidance. We are tragically mistaken if we think the Holy Ghost will simply come into our lives despite unworthiness. As the scriptures confirm, "The Spirit of the Lord will not always strive with man" (2 Nephi 26:11). Not only is righteousness a prerequisite to the companionship of the Spirit but only the faithful of God's children have the spiritual sensitivity to hear his guiding whispers and, through them, be taught the things of God.

Righteousness is not the only requirement for obtaining the guidance of the Spirit. We must also work to bring the Holy Ghost into our lives. That truth, in itself, is evidence of the pivotal role he plays, for nothing worthwhile is ever achieved easily. Were his companionship given freely, without the requirement of effort on our part, we perhaps would not cherish him as we do. Thomas Paine observed, "What we obtain too cheap, we esteem too lightly; it is dearness only that gives everything its value" (in Bartlett, *Quotations,* 271). The ability to hear the voice of the Spirit, recognize his promptings, and courageously live by his inspiration is only given to us on condition of our desire, our effort, and our righteousness.

There is something about the process of seeking—getting on our knees and supplicating the Lord—that makes us more willing and able to listen when the promptings of the Holy Ghost come. The Bible Dictionary teaches that "the object of prayer is not to change the will of God, but to secure for ourselves and for others blessings that God is already willing to grant, but that are made conditional on our asking for them. Blessings require some work or effort on our part before we can obtain them. Prayer is a form of work, and is an appointed means for obtaining the highest of all blessings" ("Prayer," 753).

Making the effort to ask is critical if we hope to receive the help of the Holy Ghost. Taking the initiative to attain the companionship of the Spirit demonstrates to the Lord how much we desire—and value—this gift and the inspiration it brings. We will not feel it fully manifested in our lives if we are not constantly pressing forward in its pursuit.

As we pray, we more fully realize the continuous flow of personal revelation available to us. Whether praying aloud on our knees or praying silently during the course of our day, the more we pray to the Lord, the more our sensitivity to the Spirit is heightened and our ability to discern his promptings is increased. President Harold B. Lee taught: "The most important thing you can do is to learn to talk to God. Talk to Him as you would talk to your father, for He is your Father and He wants you to talk to Him. He wants you to cultivate ears to listen, when He gives you the impressions of the Spirit to tell you what to do. . . . If you will cultivate an ear to hear these promptings, you will have learned to walk by the spirit of revelation" (*Teachings,* 130).

Knowing answers will come through the Holy Ghost, our spiritual ears become fine-tuned to his promptings as we pray. As we anticipate his guidance, we listen more carefully to every single whisper. Elder Henry B. Eyring said: "I have had prayers answered. Those answers were most clear when what I wanted was silenced by an overpowering need to know what God wanted. It is then that the answer from a loving Heavenly Father can be spoken to the mind by the still, small voice and can be written on the heart" ("Write," 86).

Praying with a submissive attitude indicates to the Lord true humility and opens our hearts to his will. As we approach our Heavenly Father, full of faith and truly seeking his will—first and foremost—in our lives, the Spirit will speak. Bending our will to his is an expression of our faith, a declaration to the Lord that we know his wisdom is always our most direct route to true and lasting joy.

Elder Marvin J. Ashton illustrated the principle of faith with the story of a little blind girl and her father who sat together on a train, weary from a long and difficult journey. The father's friend who was traveling with them offered to take a turn holding the little girl to give her father a rest. After the father handed his daughter to his friend and concerned that she might feel unsettled knowing she was no longer on her father's lap, he asked her, "Do you know who is holding you?" "No," she trustingly replied, "but you do" (*Cheer*, 86).

Although we may not always understand the Lord's purposes, recognizing his deep love for us assures us that we can always trust in him. During the difficult times of our lives, we can imagine the Lord asking, "Do you know why this is happening to you?" With complete faith in his infinite wisdom and his eternal perspective, we can then say to him, "No, but you do."

We see things in the limited view of mortality, but the Lord looks from the all-knowing perspective of eternity. In his wisdom, he knows what will bring about the most rapid spiritual growth in our lives, moving us as quickly as possible along the path to perfection. Many times, accelerated spiritual progression comes as a result of our trials. Despite difficulty and pain, it is in this way that challenge can greatly bless our lives.

A close friend of mine gave birth to a stillborn baby later in her life. She and her husband were devastated, but she taught me what it means to faithfully trust in the Lord's perspective despite the sting of such profound sorrow. "I know the Lord would never ask me to pass through something so difficult," she said one day in Relief Society with tears streaming down her face, "unless there was a very wise purpose in it, a purpose I just cannot see through these mortal eyes." Even in her pain, she knew the Lord must have greater purposes in mind; she knew his vision stretched far beyond her own.

No matter what hardships life may bring, the companionship of the Holy Ghost will always lessen the negative effects that accompany them and give us added strength to face them. There will come a day in our lives—or many days, for that matter—when our only answers to challenge will be found in the Spirit's whisperings. If we do not know how to hear his voice, we will face our trials alone.

Not only does the Spirit's companionship strengthen us during times of trial but it is often during our trials that we hear him most clearly. The Lord knows life's challenges will turn us to him, that our difficulties will open our eyes to truth. Speaking of the great suffering brought about by a recent Nephite-Lamanite war, the prophet Alma said, "Many were softened because of their afflictions, insomuch that they did humble themselves before God, even in the depth of humility" (Alma 62:41). During moments of great need, our hearts become soft and open to the Spirit's inspiration, for it is in those moments of personal struggle that we become acutely aware of our complete dependence on the Lord.

Although the limitations of mortality may partially conceal the purpose in trials, paying attention to the Spirit's promptings at such times will teach us much about God. Robert Browning Hamilton expressed this idea beautifully in verse:

> *I walked a mile with Pleasure.*
> *She chattered all the way,*

> *But left me none the wiser*
> *For all she had to say.*
> *I walked a mile with Sorrow,*
> *And ne'er a word said she;*
> *But oh, the things I learned from her*
> *When sorrow walked with me!*
> *("Along the Road," in* Best-Loved Poems, *2)*

Surely the Lord's heart is drawn out to us as he watches us face trials, but it is because of his love that he allows us to struggle through them. Trials are necessary parts of mortality and essential elements of spiritual growth. When difficulties try our souls, the Lord is never far from us. His charity and compassion will reach us as his loving hand is always extended toward us. As the scriptures promise, "God shall wipe away all tears from [our] eyes" (Revelation 7:17).

A fable from India tells of six men, all of them blind, who went to see an elephant. John Godfrey Saxe wrote about the visit:

> *It was six men of Indostan*
> *To learning much inclined,*
> *Who went to see the elephant*
> *(Though all of them were blind),*
> *That each by observation*
> *Might satisfy his mind.*
>
> *The First approached the elephant,*
> *And, happening to fall*
> *Against his broad and sturdy side,*

53

At once began to bawl:
"God bless me! but the elephant
Is nothing but a wall!"

The Second, feeling of the tusk,
Cried: "Ho! what have we here
So very round and smooth and sharp?
To me 'tis mighty clear
This wonder of an elephant
Is very like a spear!"

The Third approached the animal,
And, happening to take
The squirming trunk within his hands,
Thus boldly up and spake:
"I see," quoth he, "the elephant
Is very like a snake!"

The Fourth reached out his eager hand,
And felt about the knee:
"What most this wondrous beast is like
Is mighty plain," quoth he;
"'Tis clear enough the elephant
Is very like a tree."

The Fifth, who chanced to touch the ear,
Said: "E'en the blindest man
Can tell what this resembles most;
Deny the fact who can,

This marvel of an elephant
Is very like a fan!"

The Sixth no sooner had begun
About the beast to grope,
Than, seizing on the swinging tail
That fell within his scope,
"I see," quoth he, "the elephant
Is very like a rope!"

And so these men of Indostan
Disputed loud and long,
Each in his own opinion
Exceeding stiff and strong,
Though each was partly in the right,
And all were in the wrong!
   ("The Blind Men and the Elephant,"
   in Best-Loved Poems, *196–97)*

Our friends from Indostan and their experience with the elephant illustrate perfectly what happens when we lack eternal perspective. None of the men had a complete view; each saw only a part of the whole. Because of that, their perspective was partial. They were all partially correct but all completely wrong about the elephant! Like these blind men, we see only part of the picture of mortality simply because we are not yet capable of seeing the entire thing. Certainly, we cannot help but have a mortal perspective for we are, after all, mortal. Our limited vision is often clouded and our perception skewed for, like the men of Indostan, we can only see that which is directly in front of us. For them, it was the elephant. For us, it is mortality.

Our Father in Heaven, however, sees everything clearly, for his perspective is perfect and his vision without flaw. Although we, through the Spirit, gain glimpses of eternity, we will never have the capacity in our present state to see as the Lord sees. For that reason, we must rely on his vision, understanding, and guidance. We must trust in the Lord.

Nephi teaches that trust gives us strength to endure the challenges of life. In 1 Nephi 11:16–17, the Spirit of the Lord asks Nephi, "Knowest thou the condescension of God?" Nephi replies, "I know that he loveth his children; nevertheless, I do not know the meaning of all things." Nephi, at that moment, lacked the ability to fully comprehend *all* of the answers to *all* of the questions, but it caused him no worry, for he knew that God loved him. Because of that, he trusted the Lord, content in knowing that God's wisdom far exceeded his own. This understanding stilled his soul, just as it can do for each of us.

How does the Spirit manifest himself to us? How do we identify the Holy Ghost when he speaks? These questions must be answered if we are to become proficient at hearing and following his guidance. We will hear him through a quiet voice that comes into our hearts and minds. The scriptures describe the voice of the Spirit as a "still small voice, which whispereth through and pierceth all things" (D&C 85:6). Most often, this is the way the Spirit will speak. We speak figuratively of the "voice" of the Spirit, although usually there is no audible sound. It is a feeling, a thought, an impression that speaks silently to our very soul. Elder Boyd K. Packer taught:

"The Spirit does not get our attention by shouting or shaking us with a heavy hand. Rather it whispers. It caresses so gently that if we are preoccupied we may not feel it at all. . . .

"Occasionally it will press just firmly enough for us to pay heed. But most of the time, if we do not heed the gentle feeling, the Spirit will withdraw" ("Candle," 53).

Although he speaks with penetrating power, the communications of the Spirit are usually so quiet that they may be missed if we are not familiar with his voice and attentive to his whispers.

As a little girl, I remember giggling with my sister and rolling our eyes every time a certain older woman got up on fast Sunday to bear her testimony because she *always* cried. I used to wonder what she was saying that was so sad! Now that I am older, I understand. (Not only do I understand that woman but I think I have *become* that woman.) I now know that when the Spirit is present, our emotions become very tender. Most "testimony tears" come because of joy, not sadness. "We hear the words of the Lord most often by a feeling," taught President Ezra Taft Benson. "If we are humble and sensitive, the Lord will prompt us through our feelings. That is why spiritual promptings move us on occasion to great joy, sometimes to tears. Many times my emotions have been made tender and my feelings very sensitive when touched by the Spirit" (*Teachings*, 77). The Spirit brings a sweetness to life that gives birth to intense joy, reassuring peace, and very often—tears.

Most people would agree that we possess five senses, five ways to discern what is happening in the physical world around us. These are the abilities to taste, touch, smell, see, and hear. Few of us need any explanation of these senses, for they have been a part of us since the day we came into this world. The ability to recognize the communications of the Holy Ghost, however, requires the development of another of our senses— one we are not as well acquainted with.

It is a spiritual sense that puts us in tune with the divine and gives us the capability to discern spiritual promptings. Brigham Young University professor Robert J. Matthews once said, "We are not simply mortals having an occasional spiritual experience. We are very old spirits, children of heavenly parents, having a mortal experience" (*Writings*, 502). It is true! Because we were spiritual beings long before we were mortal, we were given this spiritual sense eons ago. It has always been a part of us.

A friend's daughter, after receiving her temple endowment, remarked, "I felt like I was being reminded of things I already knew." Truly, she was, just as developing our spiritual sense in mortality is simply being reminded of a spiritual connection we have always had. President Joseph F. Smith taught: "All those salient truths which come home so forcibly to the head and heart seem but the awakening of the memories of the spirit. Can we know anything here that we did not know before we came? Are not the means of knowledge in the first estate equal to those of this? I think that the spirit, before and after this probation, possesses greater facilities, aye, manifold greater, for the acquisition of knowledge, than while manacled and shut up in the prison-house of mortality.

" . . . But in coming here, we forgot all, that our agency might be free indeed, to choose good or evil, that we might merit the reward of our own choice and conduct. But by the power of the Spirit, in the redemption of Christ, through obedience, we often catch a spark from the awakened memories of the immortal soul, which lights up our whole being as with the glory of our former home" (*Doctrine,* 13–14).

Certainly, that is why we feel so comfortable when the Holy Ghost is upon us. We have known him before. As we become reacquainted with him in mortality, it is a familiar voice we hear. When we feel the Spirit's influence, we feel content, relaxed, and serene. We are spiritually and intellectually engaged. That explains how we can bask in the warmth of a spiritual experience and never tire of it. When the Spirit is present, it is as if time stands still.

The Spirit creates a place of complete peace in a world of struggle, bringing spiritual safety in times of great spiritual trial. He is our "light in the wilderness" (1 Nephi 17:13), "a banner upon the high mountain" (Isaiah 13:2), in times when valley fog clouds our view. Once we experience his influence and feel the transforming power he brings, we then begin to hunger for his constant companionship. After feeling what it is like to live *with* him, we are determined to never live a day *without* him or

foolishly try to make it on our own. The more we feel his influence, the more we recognize how much we truly need it and the
more we desire to receive it. We feel comfort in his touch. We
seek him, for we know he represents the Lord in our lives. When
the Spirit prompts us, it is as though we hear the voice of the
Lord saying to us personally, "Ye shall be led towards the promised land; and ye shall know that it is by me that ye are led"
(1 Nephi 17:13).

Every sense we possess can be more fully developed through
effort and time. My husband had a job that required him to hit
a baseball coming toward him at an extremely high speed. They
say it takes close to two thousand at-bats in the minor leagues
to hit major league pitching and just as many to see if a player
is even capable of doing it. When Dale signed his first professional baseball contract, by his own admission, he could never
have hit major league pitching. It took him years of practice—
day after day of repetition—to be successful. Practicing
increased his skills, certainly. But it did even more than that. It
fine-tuned his senses. For example, the half second it takes for
the ball to travel from the pitcher's hand to home plate seems
to most of us not nearly enough time for any batter to evaluate
a pitch and decide whether he should swing. If he has to stop
and think about it, he will miss every time. But the experience
gained through practice teaches him to identify certain pitches
instinctively and react to them, adjusting his timing to (hope-
fully) hit one. His senses are enhanced and strengthened as he
puts forth consistent effort and gains greater experience.

When I first learned to bake cookies, I set the timer for exactly the number of minutes specified in the recipe—no more, no less. When the timer rang, I took the cookies out of the oven. Whether they were done, underdone, or even burned, I never varied the time. Now, many years and inedible cookies later, effort and experience have taught me that I can actually smell when it's time to take them out. Somewhere along the line, my sense of smell has become my most trusted timer. As talents go, it's certainly nothing to write home about. It does, however, teach a valuable lesson: We each have the ability to cultivate, enhance, and refine our individual senses. They can become extremely reliable guides in our lives.

The mother of young children, able to hear soft footsteps in the hallway at night; the golfer, able to focus in on a little hole in the ground from a great distance away; the chef who can distinguish different spices in a dish simply by tasting it—all have keenly developed senses. Some may believe these abilities come naturally, but generally speaking, the bearer has earned them through extraordinary effort. Those lacking in one sense often have extreme sensitivity in another. Those without sight, for example, train themselves to rely on other senses—perhaps hearing or touch—to compensate for the lack of sight. As a result, those senses become extremely sharp and well-defined.

Increasing our spiritual sense is no different. As with most things, time and practice yield experience when understanding the workings of the Spirit, experience that teaches us how to hear his promptings and keep the lines of communication open, free from static and interference. To fine-tune our spiritual sense, we must listen carefully, over and over again, teaching ourselves to recognize the subtle characteristics of the Spirit's voice and become aware of the times and places we hear him the most clearly. We must create an environment where he can be heard and then immerse ourselves in it. As we do, our spiritual sense expands, and this wonderful gift becomes fully operational in our lives.

No matter how proficient we become at receiving communication from the Holy Ghost, we must find quiet moments in our lives if we hope to hear his promptings. "To be spiritually honest," wrote Joseph Fielding McConkie, "is to listen for and accept the quiet whisperings of the Spirit. Although the Ten Commandments were thundered from the mountaintop, the more sacred doctrines are manifest in temples, closets, and quiet places" (*Symbolism*, 248).

Finding those "quiet places" is only possible as we make a conscious effort to discover them. They will not simply *happen*. A friend of ours finds his quiet moments at 4:00 A.M., waking up to study and ponder in the silence of those early-morning hours. It may not be the ideal hour of the day for most of us, but for him, it's the best time to find the quiet solitude that invites the promptings of the Holy Ghost into his life in a profound way.

From cell phones to car radios to busy households and twenty-four-hour-a-day news, we live in a noisy world. Most of us have a difficult time finding any quiet at all in our day; to find it often may seem an impossible task. Gerald N. Lund spoke of lessening the noise in our lives:

"One of the most important things you can do when you are searching to reduce inner noise in your life is to take time to ponder and reflect. Get away from the bustle of life. Find a quiet place and take time to simply sit and think, to listen to your thoughts and feelings, to open yourself to the promptings of the Spirit. Note what the following prophets said they were doing prior to receiving important revelations. Nephi: 'I sat pondering in mine heart' (1 Ne. 11:1). Joseph Smith and Sidney Rigdon: 'While we meditated upon these things' (D&C 76:19). Joseph F. Smith: 'I sat in my room pondering over the scriptures; and reflecting' (D&C 138:1–2). Joseph Smith: 'My mind was called up to serious reflection. . . . I reflected . . . again and again [upon the words of James]' (JS-H 1:8, 12)" (*Writings,* 284).

It is in those quiet, thoughtful hours that we will hear the strongest promptings and feel the most distinct nudgings of the Holy Ghost. Like the Prophet Joseph, it is during our moments of quiet reflection that the Lord—through the Spirit—will speak. In order to prepare our hearts to hear him, the Lord gives us this counsel: "Be still and know that I am God" (D&C 101:16).

Most of us have wondered from time to time if we truly are receiving answers to our prayers, for answers are often difficult to hear. Promptings come more easily than we may suspect, but the noise we allow into our lives causes interference and keeps us from recognizing the inspiration we seek. It makes sense that the still, small voice is best heard when we are still and quiet. We certainly cannot hear a whisper if something else is shouting in our ear.

Perhaps not realizing it, we often contribute to the noise in our lives by giving our time to things that are unnecessary and relatively unimportant. We seem determined to fill every waking moment—and even some when we should be sleeping—with things to do. But it is not only our overflowing schedules which create a disconnection between us and the Holy Ghost. The voices of the world constantly call out to us, confusing us as they create chatter in our heads and unrest in our hearts. Any noise that interferes with our ability to hear the Spirit must be quieted if we hope to live by his soft and gentle whispers.

Although the world typically values that which is temporary and fleeting, as children of God we must learn to judge more wisely. It has been said, "That which you give your time to, you give your life to." Logical? Yes. But do we stop long enough to internalize the truth of those words and recognize that many things we purchase with our precious time may not be worth the cost? As we reach the end of our lives and look back with true perspective, how disappointed we will be if we discover time we should have spent wisely was frittered away.

I've thought of this often as I have considered a dear friend who recently lost his life to cancer. He lived a life of honor, continually under the influence of the Spirit and wholly dedicated to the Lord. Charity was a way of life for him. Even during his times of extreme pain and difficulty, he was serving those around him. During the last weeks of his life, I answered my phone one day and heard his weak voice on the other end. I was surprised because I knew how sick he was. I good-naturedly told him he could hang up the phone and go back to bed, implying that he could finally stop thinking only of others and spend a little time doing something for himself. But, no, he wanted to tell me something about my seventeen-year-old son that had impressed him, so he had picked up the phone and called. No one would have known—or blamed him—if he hadn't acted on that prompting.

That's just the kind of person he was. He knew that phone call would mean so much to me and, caring little for his own difficult state, took the time to do something kind for someone else. His many acts of love and service could never be measured, at least not in earthly terms. I have never known anyone else like him, and doubt that I ever will. The lyrics of a popular song speak of the ways we might live differently if we knew we were dying, but even the certainty of our friend's approaching death did not change the way he lived—no sudden course corrections or fast-track repentance for him. No, he was living the life of a true disciple long before he ever knew he was sick. Following the Savior's example, he, too, "went about doing good" (Acts 10:38) and lived every moment to its fullest, despite the short-ened life he was given. Although prepared to accept God's will, he certainly did not want to die. What he would have given, what he would have traded, for just one more day—one more hour or minute or second—with those he loved so dearly in this life.

And here *we* are, sometimes living our days as if we have a never-ending supply of them, often tied up in things that seem so important but will be forgotten so soon, wasting precious moments and God-given energy on things which have no eternal significance. Do we realize how precious our time is, or will it only become truly valuable when we know it is about to end? And what about those of us who will not have that foreknowledge but will leave mortality in an instant with absolutely no warning?

Because our days truly are numbered, we must make judgments about which things deserve our energy, for so many things continually call out to us for our time. How tempting it can be to follow the world and seek after counterfeit treasures that possess no lasting value. We must choose wisely so we need never look back with regret. Our friend's life—and death—are constant reminders to us of the value of every day and the sacred nature of the time we are given. We must cherish each moment, for one of the moments ahead will be our last.

The story is told of a man who visited an art gallery and purchased an expensive painting. He took it home and searched for the perfect place to hang it. As hard as he tried, however, he could not find a spot that seemed just right. In frustration he returned the painting to the gallery, explaining that, although he loved it, he simply had no room for it in his home. Surprised, the curator looked him in the eye and gave him this wise advice:

"If you really love this painting, this is what you must do: Go home. Take everything out of your house. Hang up the painting. Then put back into your house only the things that fit."

Like this man, we must rid our lives of the things that matter least, making room for those which matter most. As we do, we will discover peace-filled moments of quiet communion with the Holy Ghost and forge a true and genuine friendship with him.

In the premortal realm, we wholeheartedly embraced the plan of our Father in Heaven. Despite the risks, we agreed to the terms set before us and readied ourselves to begin the adventure of mortality. Trial and challenge would inevitably come, but the eternal perspective we then possessed must have quieted our fears, for the threat of difficulty did not deter us from accepting our long-awaited chance at eventual godhood. We anxiously came to earth, confident in our ability to return. Certainly we gained great comfort as we that learned the gift of the Holy Ghost would be available to us. Knowing he could walk by our side surely gave us confidence as we considered the inevitable struggles ahead. Pain, disappointment, sickness, and heartbreak would certainly come, but the anticipation of the Holy Ghost's comforting hand gave us great strength.

Although a veil of forgetfulness has been drawn across our mortal eyes, we are allowed occasional glimmers of memory and brief but vivid impressions of our life prior to our physical birth. Author Lucy Maud Montgomery wrote:

"It has always seemed to me, ever since early childhood,

amid all the commonplaces of life, I was very near to a kingdom of ideal beauty. Between it and me hung only a thin veil. I could never draw it quite aside, but sometimes a wind fluttered it and I caught a glimpse of the enchanting realm beyond—only a glimpse—but those glimpses have always made life worthwhile" (Montgomery, *Anne,* xiii-xiv, quoted in Maxwell, *Not My Will,* 9–10).

At times, the door between us and the spirit world seems slightly ajar, and the feelings that exist there seem to flood into our lives. These are the moments when the Holy Ghost is speaking; these are the occasions when he reminds us of our heavenly home. There is never a time we feel closer to our Father in Heaven than when the Holy Ghost is with us.

We must recognize the Holy Ghost for what he is: our lifeline to heaven. A personage of spirit, the Holy Ghost speaks to *our* spirits, helping us navigate the troubled tides of mortality. He guides us with gentle nudgings, prompts us to make slight adjustments in course, inspires us to places we would not go alone, and burns truth deep into our hearts.

All who have received the gift of the Holy Ghost are capable of receiving his constant direction; all can qualify for his tender and attentive care. His influence in our lives is of unequalled value. As the intermediary between us and our Father in Heaven, he offers us every good gift the Father has to give. To live without him in mortality would be like swimming the English Channel wearing a backpack filled with bricks. The experience would be miserable, and we would never reach our final destination.

As children of God, we know that listening to the whisperings of the Spirit will protect us from the spiritual hazards of the world. With him, our course is sure. We need not rely on the whims of a wayward society, for we are led by a never-changing God. We need not rely on the opinions of men; we are given the word of God to answer the questions of life. We need not rely on the understanding of the world; we are given the Holy Ghost to open our eyes to truth and bless our lives with peace.

STEP FIVE

Find quiet moments in your day. Schedule them, if necessary. Wake up ten minutes earlier if you must. Cut something else out of your day if you can. Give yourself time to just sit. Think. Ponder. Pray. But most of all, listen carefully for the whisperings of the Spirit.

From the scripture journal of Joseph Smith:

> *I speak unto you with my voice, even the voice of my Spirit.*
> —DOCTRINE AND COVENANTS 97:1

> *Thus saith the still small voice, which whispereth through and pierceth all things.*
> —DOCTRINE AND COVENANTS 85:6

From the scripture journal of Nephi:

> *He hath spoken unto you in a still small voice.*
> —1 NEPHI 17:45

CHAPTER SIX

THE HOLY GHOST SPEAKS TO US

By the Spirit are all things made known.
1 NEPHI 22:2

I was the last of all my girlfriends to be married. I still remember wondering how they knew when it was right, how they had enough confidence in their decision to actually say yes to a marriage proposal. Hoping I would have to make the same decision someday, I asked several of them how they received their answer. What did it sound like? How did they know it was the Spirit speaking? They all responded in much the same way with almost exactly the same words: "I just *knew*." I have to admit, I never understood that answer. What did it even mean? Maybe they hadn't really received an answer at all, I thought, and just wanted to satisfy my curiosity by saying *something*. Their simple description of what I thought must have been an earth-shattering revelation always frustrated me. I wanted specifics!

The day my husband proposed to me, I suddenly understood. I heard the explanation—and my answer—in a silent voice that warmed me with peace, comfort, and confirmation. There was no way to explain it; no way to repeat the actual words that were said, for they were words without form or sound. It was a language I was just beginning to learn, but I understood it clearly. Because it was meant only for me, it was heard only by me, spoken in a way I would recognize as a witness from the Holy Ghost. Since that time, I have occasionally been asked how I knew my decision to marry my husband was the right one. I always think back on that day when I was spoken to in the language of the Lord, and I always reply, "I just *knew*."

Since the time of Babel mankind has lived in confusion. Have you ever tried to communicate with someone who did not speak your language? You can speak as slowly and clearly as you like, but the other person will still not understand a word you say. Our oldest son was called to serve his mission in Japan and in the Missionary Training Center had a companion from Peru. The companion, of course, spoke only Spanish. Our son spoke only English. As you can imagine, communicating with each other was challenging, particularly since the only language they shared was the fragmented Japanese they were just beginning to learn.

A few years after they had both returned home, we sat in

our living room with our son, his companion, and his companion's parents, who were visiting from Peru. We did not speak a language in common with them, which soon became a major challenge. To talk to them, we would tell our son, in English, what we wanted to say. He would repeat it in Japanese to his companion, who would repeat it in Spanish to his parents. The process would then reverse itself as they answered. After a few times of this, we all began to laugh. Not only was it a very tedious and inefficient way to communicate but it was extremely funny to watch.

There are nearly seven thousand languages spoken in the world today (*Enthnologue*). Although each of us has our own language, even understanding our native tongue does not come naturally. It must be practiced and learned by trial and error. When our children were small, it was quite entertaining to watch them as they learned to speak—and comprehend—the English language.

One son, figuring he would practice the most important words first, had only four words in his vocabulary: *football, baseball, basketball,* and *golf.* He would repeat them over and over again, in no particular order, entertaining himself for incredibly long periods of time.

When medical tests showed our eighth child was a girl, after seven boys in a row, our then four-year-old son could not remember the word *sister*—it had never been in his vocabulary before. Instead, he would just tell people he was going to have a "girl-brother."

After deciding to leave Atlanta, we told our children we were moving to Utah. Our two-year-old looked puzzled and said, "ME-tah?"

"No. Utah," we replied.

Looking exasperated, he said, "That's what I said! ME-tah!"

Another son, knowing his older brother's baptism would be at the church in a font filled with water, loved to tell people his brother was getting "bath-tized." It made perfect sense to him!

And one of the funniest questions we've ever heard was when another child asked, in all seriousness, if Mickey Rooney invented macaroni. Eventually, all of our children learned to speak English, but not without work—and a lot of laughs!

Learning any language is a process. Gaining proficiency takes time, effort, and patience. There are no shortcuts. To communicate with someone, we must know their language. Language can often be an obstacle, but it can also build bridges that connect people, determine culture, and identify exactly who we are. Even when living within the same community, we usually separate ourselves according to our language. It simply makes life easier. In these ways, the language we speak becomes a defining element of our lives.

What is the language of the Lord, and how do we learn to understand it? How do we know when it is he who is speaking? How do we recognize his voice?

The scriptures teach that the Holy Ghost is the intermediary between us and our Father in Heaven. Through him, we are shown the "will of the Lord, . . . the mind of the Lord, . . . the word of the Lord, . . . the voice of the Lord, and the power of God unto salvation" (D&C 68:4). In his epistle to his beloved son Moroni, Mormon wrote, "The word of the Lord came to me by the power of the Holy Ghost" (Moroni 8:7). In 2 Nephi 32:3, we not only learn that "angels speak by the power of the Holy Ghost" but also that "they speak the words of Christ." The words spoken by the Holy Ghost are, indeed, the words of the Savior to us. Because of this truth, we must become familiar with the many ways the Holy Ghost speaks if we hope to learn to hear God's voice and know his will in our lives.

As we understand the specific ways the Holy Ghost comes to us, we will be more likely to recognize him when he does. Most of the world is oblivious to his presence, and for this reason, God's "power . . . looks small unto the understanding of men" (Ether 3:5). But to those who have received the gift of the Holy Ghost by priesthood power through the laying on of hands, God's power looks mighty and is constantly revealed.

There are many ways the Lord, through the Holy Ghost, may speak to us. He communicates in dreams, although not all dreams are necessarily revelation. He speaks through living prophets, giving us counsel directly from our Father in Heaven. Doctrine and Covenants 1:38 teaches, "Whether by mine own voice or by the voice of my servants, it is the same." Gaining a testimony of this truth opens our ears and our hearts to the prophets, knowing they truly speak the words of God.

The Lord also speaks to us through the words of others as they are moved upon by the Holy Ghost. The Bible Dictionary states, "When a person speaks by the power of the Holy Ghost that same power carries a conviction of the truth into the heart of the hearer" ("Holy Ghost," 704). The prophet Nephi taught, "When a man speaketh by the power of the Holy Ghost the power of the Holy Ghost carrieth it unto the hearts of the children of men" (2 Nephi 33:1). In this way the Spirit can speak to us through someone else and touch our hearts through the words another person is inspired to say. Doctrine and Covenants 50:22 explains further: "Wherefore, he that preacheth and he that receiveth, understand one another, and both are edified and rejoice together." When we earn the companionship of the Spirit, we can receive truth and act as a worthy vessel to carry that truth to others.

How do we recognize the whisperings of the Spirit?

"The scriptures indicate that manifestations of the Spirit come to the mind in a variety of ways," explained Elder L. Lionel Kendrick. "They come as an enlightenment, just as scriptures seem to be illuminated with understanding. They may come in the form of instant recall of things or as a clear audible voice. Sometimes they come by way of counsel from leaders. They come in dreams, visions, and visitations" (*Speeches*, 257).

Joseph Smith spoke of other ways the Holy Ghost may come. He said, "A person may profit by noticing the first intimation of the spirit of revelation; for instance, when you feel pure intelligence flowing into you, it may give you sudden strokes of ideas" (*Teachings*, 151, quoted in Packer, "Personal," 60).

There are certainly occasions when the Lord speaks in miraculous ways, but most often he is heard through the soft and gentle voice of the Holy Ghost. Typically, His words find their way into our hearts through something as simple as a thought or a feeling. "The burning bushes, the smoking mountains, . . . the Cumorahs, and the Kirtlands were realities," said President Spencer W. Kimball, "but they were the exceptions. The great volume of revelation came to Moses and to Joseph and comes to today's prophet in the less spectacular way—that of deep impressions, without spectacle or glamour or dramatic events" (Munich Area Conference Report, 1973, 77).

No matter how the Spirit is manifest in our lives, no matter what his chosen method of communication, we must develop the ability to recognize him. Whether his promptings come as a dream, as a talk in general conference, or as an idea that comes suddenly to our minds, we must be ever watchful. If we are not sensitive and alert, we may miss him altogether. He will not announce his arrival; it is our responsibility to discern when he is near.

In the beginning the Lord always speaks gently. His beckoning call is one of invitation, not scolding or judgment. In meekness he bids us follow; with loving persuasion he entreats us to obey. The choice must be ours, however, for agency must be allowed, and eternal law cannot be broken. The scriptures reveal times when the Lord's patience has been tried by the disobedience of his children. At these moments he speaks with a stronger voice in a different language. His voice then is louder and very difficult to ignore. C. S. Lewis described it as a "megaphone to rouse a deaf world" (*Pain,* 91). And so it is.

God, as our Father, must occasionally awaken his sleeping children with much more than a mere whisper. He must use a voice they will hear; he must speak in a language to which they will respond. There are times when the Lord becomes stern, even angry, for the purpose of bringing his children back to him. Doctrine and Covenants 63:32 says, "I, the Lord, am angry with the wicked; I am holding my Spirit from the inhabitants of the earth." And Moses 6:27 says, "Repent, for thus saith the Lord: I am angry with this people, and my fierce anger is kindled against them." Deuteronomy 9:8 tells of a time the people "provoked the Lord to wrath": 1 Nephi 17:35 records: "The fulness of the wrath of God was upon them." Job 21:17 gives some insight into the results: "God distributeth sorrows in his anger."

This language is familiar to every righteous parent, for there are times when children must be roused from spiritual slumber. True Christlike love redeems others, and it is that kind of love which prompts parents to awaken their children when necessary. In his infinite wisdom and because he loves his children, it is often necessary for God to firmly warn those who are not otherwise listening. To his children who continually disregard the promptings of the Holy Ghost or through their own wickedness squelch the light of Christ which is given to all men, the Lord will eventually speak a language they will understand. The reason for this is recorded in Helaman 15:3: "He chastened them because he loveth them."

Nephi was overcome with sorrow because of the wickedness of his people. It was a time of many wars in the land. Fearing the Lord would allow these wars and their accompanying tribulations to come upon his people to compel them to repent, Nephi pleaded with him to instead send a famine to the land to do the job. The Lord answered Nephi's prayers and sent a famine, which eventually brought his people to their knees in humility and led them to repentance. Being familiar with the ways of God, Nephi feared that the Lord was about to speak a language that his people, in their wickedness, would understand—the language of war and destruction. Because Nephi "did cry unto the Lord" (Helaman 11:3), asking him to speak instead the language of famine among his people and thus spare many lives, we are told that "it was done" (Helaman 11:5).

The Lord uses yet another language to attract our attention. "He often employs the forces of nature, in the thunder storm, in lightning, in famine, in earthquake, in . . . one of the forces of nature, to bring to the understanding and attention of his children that which they would not understand in more gentle tones," said Elder Heber Q. Hale. "For 120 years God spoke through his servant Noah to the children of his great world family, as they existed at that time. They failed to respond to the spoken word; they failed to respond to the word of tradition, as it came down to them from their father Adam, and so God must then speak through some voice of nature that his word might be heard and his mandates obeyed; and the clouds of heaven gathered, and burst forth and scattered rain upon the earth until the low places were filled, until floods dashed upon the streets and into the valleys, and the people began to flee from their homes to the high places. Noah had withdrawn with his family into the ark, and with him the chosen beasts of the field. When the people perceiving their peril cried out unto God, 'Save us from this peril,' it was too late; their opportunity for salvation had passed" (Conference Report, Apr. 1917, 107).

Just as obedience always provides safe shelter from the storms of life, wickedness never does, for "the devil will not support his children at the last day, but doth speedily drag them down to hell" (Alma 30:60). Disobedience always yields despair, fulfilling Satan's objective that "all men might be miserable like unto himself" (2 Nephi 2:27). Elder Hale continued: "When the morning broke and it was discovered in the homes of the Egyptians that their first born sons were slain, then they understood. God had at last spoken a language that pagan Egypt understood and obeyed, and Israel went forth miraculously delivered from the hands of the Egyptians" (Conference Report, Apr. 1917, 108).

Whatever the method of communication, the Lord has always spoken to his children. Sometime we listen; sometimes we do not. Although we may choose our response, we cannot choose the consequences that follow. The scriptures are filled with examples of each: those who have wisely heeded his voice, and those who have foolishly neglected it. Unfortunately for the spiritually oblivious, there is no safe haven, for sooner or later the price for disobedience must be paid. But those who wisely choose to listen earn the trust of a loving God and promised blessings along the way.

STEP SIX

Find a printed talk from the last general conference. As you read it, list in the margin every bit of instruction and advice given. Record it in your scripture journal along with your testimony of living prophets, who speak by the power of the Holy Ghost. The Holy Ghost then testifies to us of the truth of their words.

From the scripture journal of Alma:

For the Lord God hath made them manifest unto me by his Holy Spirit.

—ALMA 5:46

From the scripture journal of Moroni:

And when ye shall receive these things, I would exhort you that ye would ask God, the Eternal Father, in the name of Christ, if these things are not true; and if ye shall ask with a sincere heart, with real intent, having faith in Christ, he will manifest the truth of it unto you, by the power of the Holy Ghost.

And by the power of the Holy Ghost ye may know the truth of all things.

—MORONI 10:4–5

From the scripture journal of Joseph Smith:

Yea, behold, I will tell you in your mind and in your heart, by the Holy Ghost, which shall come upon you and which shall dwell in your heart.

—DOCTRINE AND COVENANTS 8:2

CHAPTER SEVEN

HIS INFLUENCE WILL BLESS US

For they that are wise . . . have taken
the Holy Spirit for their guide.
DOCTRINE AND COVENANTS 45:57

No discussion of the blessings offered by the Holy Ghost can be complete, just as any attempt to credit him for all he does is inevitably lacking. Not only is it impossible to name the many ways he touches us, but no mortal words can fully explain the mission he performs on our behalf.

The Spirit is a holy visitor whose presence is not always recognized. It is simply not possible for us as imperfect mortals to fully predict or comprehend the profound effect he can have on our lives. Because we do not always know when he is near, we are, no doubt, largely unaware of the many times he intervenes on our behalf. He plays a larger role in our lives than we may suspect, and the far-reaching effects of his companionship are more central to our mortal existence than we may know. For example, at times when we are kind, we may not realize that the influence of the Holy Ghost is the source of that kindness. When we forgive others, we may fail to understand that our compassionate nature is not our own doing but the reflection of the change brought upon us by the Holy Ghost, which makes us more forgiving of our fellowman.

If it were possible to recognize the full extent of his influence, we would fall to our knees in gratitude for all that he makes possible in mortality. Elder Dallin H. Oaks taught of the incredible scope of the Spirit's influence: "That Spirit—the Holy Ghost—is our comforter, our direction finder, our communicator, our interpreter, our witness, and our purifier—our infallible guide and sanctifier for our mortal journey toward eternal life" ("Always," 61).

The Spirit's mission clearly involves the perfecting of God's children. It is a task whose accomplishment hinges on our ability to bring him into our lives and keep him there. Walking with him is an unequaled opportunity and a profound privilege. What we often fail to realize, however, is that receiving this gift bestows upon us much more than privilege; it places squarely on our shoulders great responsibility in our quest to become more like God.

It has been said, "Where much is given, much is expected." True enough, but that is not a completely accurate statement. The scripture actually reads: "For of him unto whom much is given much is *required*" (D&C 82:3; emphasis added). There is a great difference between expecting and requiring, which illuminates the depth of our accountability in regard to the Holy Ghost. We who possess the gift of his companionship are not just *expected* to live by his whisperings; we are *required* to do so. The Lord, through his servants, admonishes us to this end. Elder Brigham Young Jr. taught, "We should live, and it is our privilege to so live, as to be operated upon by the influences of the Spirit of God through all our labors until the whisperings of that Spirit shall be constantly with us" (Conference Report, Apr. 1880, 31).

Amulek pleaded with the wayward Zoramites to realize—and reverse—the tragedy that had beset them: They were unworthy and living without the Spirit in their lives. He urged them "that ye contend no more against the Holy Ghost, but that ye receive it, . . . and that ye live in thanksgiving daily, for the many mercies and blessings which [God] doth bestow upon you" (Alma 34:38). Further investigation into the word *contend* in this scripture reveals it to mean "loss of the Holy Ghost" (Alma 34:38, note a), which tells us much about the Zoramites' spiritual state, for they had given up the blessings of the Spirit, and Amulek knew they had made a tragic mistake.

We must not make the same mistake, for without the companionship of the Holy Ghost we will not only fail in our pursuit of exaltation but we will also lose available and promised blessings intended specifically for us. Through the Prophet Joseph Smith the Lord names one such blessing, as he gives an invitation and a promise: "Walk in the meekness of my Spirit, and you shall have peace in me" (D&C 19:23). He gently commands us to humbly follow the guidance of the Holy Ghost and offers the promise of peace to all who will do so. Peace truly is the ultimate prize given to all who live by the light of heaven. President Brigham Young taught of the great need for peace as well as its grand effect in our lives:

"Thrust a man into prison and bind him with chains, and then let him be filled with the comfort and with the glory of eternity, and that prison is a palace to him. Again, let a man be seated upon a throne with power and dominion in this world, ruling his millions and millions and without that peace which flows from the Lord of Hosts—without that contentment and joy that comes from heaven, his palace is a prison; his life is a burden to him; he lives in fear, in dread, and in sorrow. But when a person is filled with the peace and power of God, all is right with him" (*Discourses*, 33).

Every commandment the Lord gives is ultimately to bless his children. Many commandments require great sacrifice and, very often, blessings come only after much work and struggle. In regard to the Holy Ghost, however, the Lord asks so little in return and stands ready to bless us if only we will do our part. The rewards are readily available. To observe his generosity in this matter brings a solid testimony that he actively desires to open the windows of heaven on our behalf. President Brigham Young said: "If the Latter-day Saints will walk up to their privileges, and exercise faith in the name of Jesus Christ, and live in the enjoyment of the fullness of the Holy Ghost constantly day by day, there is nothing on the face of the earth that they could ask for, that would not be given to them" (*Journal of Discourses,* 11:114). Nothing but good awaits those who obtain the companionship of the Spirit and learn to live by his every word.

We all need the Holy Ghost. It is as if we are travelers in a foreign land, dependent on a local guide who knows the area, is familiar with the culture, and speaks our language as well as his own. Why would we ever try to get along without him, unless being lost and confused was our ultimate goal? Spiritually speaking, we are in a similar circumstance. This earth is not our home. We are visitors here, dependent on a divine guide—a spiritual interpreter—to help us find our way back to our Father in Heaven, who anticipates our return. What reason could possibly justify our failure to listen to this divine friend? Are we complacent or neglectful, or do we simply forget to pay attention? Ignorance may sometimes be bliss, but with the gift of the Holy Ghost, ignorance is spiritual suicide. If we were skydiving from a plane, would we ignore the parachute strapped to our back? Would we let ourselves forget it was there? Certainly not, for doing so would lead to devastating consequences. In a similar way, living without the Holy Ghost will always threaten our spiritual safety. Overlooking his influence will always lead to a miserable landing. We simply cannot forget he is there or lose sight of the spiritual protection he provides.

The scriptures and modern revelation teach much about how the Holy Ghost works, giving us knowledge that helps us recognize him when he is present. Elder Parley P. Pratt beautifully described the remarkable blessings afforded us by the Holy Ghost: "The gift of the Holy Ghost," he said, "quickens all the intellectual faculties, increases, enlarges, expands and purifies all the natural passions and affections; and adapts them, by the gift of wisdom, to their lawful use. It inspires, develops, cultivates and matures all the fine-toned sympathies, joys, tastes, kindred feelings and affections of our nature. It inspires virtue, kindness, goodness, tenderness, gentleness and charity. It develops beauty of person, form and features. It tends to health, vigor, animation and social feeling. It invigorates all the faculties of the physical and intellectual man. It strengthens, and gives tone to the nerves. In short, it is, as it were, marrow to the bone, joy to the heart, light to the eyes, music to the ears, and life to the whole being" (*Key,* 101).

The Holy Ghost awakens us to life and moves us from who we are to who the Lord intends us to be. Clearly, we can never hope to reach the potential buried deep within us if we do not learn to rely on the Spirit's perceptive guidance. Only our Father in Heaven sees exactly who we can become, and only through the Holy Ghost can he show us exactly who that is.

There is no area of our lives that the Holy Ghost cannot touch, no part of us the Holy Ghost cannot improve upon. There is no limit to what he can do or how often he can do it. His power and influence are limitless.

Our fallen, mortal state demands constant and consistent course correction, and for that reason, the Spirit is always available. Living in this world will never be easy, and for that reason, the Spirit is always on call. We are the only ones who can keep the Holy Ghost from guiding us. "There is no reason in the world," said President Joseph Fielding Smith, "if men would only hearken to the whisperings of the Spirit of the Lord and seek as he would have them seek for the knowledge and under-standing of the gospel of Jesus Christ, for them not to find it—no reason, except the hardness of their hearts and their love of the world. 'Knock, and it shall be opened unto you'" (Conference Report, Apr. 1951, 59). We greatly impede our progression when we do not seek the Holy Ghost for, as this promise explains, we *will* find him if our desire is deep and our hearts are turned to God.

When spiritual truth is revealed, our spiritual understanding is deepened and our lives are changed. The awe-inspiring moments when we experience this manifestation are equaled only by the chance to observe them happen in the life of another person. One day as our oldest son walked the streets of Japan, he and his missionary companion approached a man and handed him a picture of Christ, introducing themselves as his representatives. To their complete astonishment, the man had never heard the name of Jesus Christ before, much less seen a representation of him. Had the man said he did not believe in Jesus Christ or did not worship him, that would not have been such a surprise. But that he had been completely without this truth in his life was incomprehensible to these two young Latter-day Saint missionaries from America.

They stood there for several minutes with the man, bearing

testimony of the reality of the Savior and his divine mission. Light began to fill the man's eyes as they saw the Holy Ghost bear witness of the truth he had just heard. What a thrill to actually see the Spirit at work, to recognize his presence and understand exactly what was taking place. The Holy Ghost had come. While there, he planted in this man's heart the very beginnings of the seeds of faith. Seeing his converting power was a testimony-building experience for those two missionaries, one that is repeated on street corners and in mud huts and on living room sofas all around the world every day of every year as the Spirit whispers the testimony of truth and gathers the elect.

Following promptings of the Holy Ghost is only possible if we consistently ignore and flatly reject the teachings of the world that are contrary to the gospel of Jesus Christ. President Thomas S. Monson said: "Cunningly positioned are those clever pied pipers of sin beckoning here or there. Do not be deceived. Pause to pray. Listen to that still, small voice which speaks to the depths of our souls the Master's gentle invitation: 'Come, follow me'" ("Sailing," 4).

Left to ourselves, we may be influenced by those who inhabit the great and spacious building—pointing, mocking, and manipulating us into following their chosen path, a path leading only to sorrow and spiritual death. The Holy Ghost offers protection from those who love sin more than they love us and who would gladly lead us astray. For example, in an effort to teach our children to judge more wisely the music they listen to, we remind them that many in the music industry do not care about *them* as much as they care about *money.* As a matter of fact, most do not care about our children at all. This fact is evidenced by their lack of concern for the powerful and often destructive influence of their music on a generation of impressionable young men and women. Their primary interest, instead, is how much money vulgarity can generate and how rich they can become while sailing on a river of filth. We remind our children that they must be wise. If we are true to the whisperings of the Spirit, we will not be misled. He will direct us away from those whose true interest in us lies only in the truth that misery does indeed love company.

Nephi taught of the Spirit's ability to keep us on a righteous path: "If ye will . . . receive the Holy Ghost, it will show unto you all things what ye should do" (2 Nephi 32:5). Because no two days, no two situations, and no two people are exactly the same, we need the inspiration of the Holy Ghost, which comes to us in individual and very personal ways. Elder Neal A. Maxwell explained:

"Of meeting and coping with such real and recurring challenges in the kingdom, one basic fact is paramount: There can be no all-purpose handbook to cover all human situations with a page for every problem; each of us must develop his own responses to such dilemmas, and those responses must be given to us by the Holy Ghost, who is the unerring guide in telling us 'all things' we need to do" (*Press,* 38).

The Holy Ghost empowers us with courage to live the commandments of God. Through him we also gain the ability to avoid sin. President Lorenzo Snow promised, "If we are careful to listen to [the Spirit's] whisperings, and understand the nature of its language, we may avoid much trouble and serious difficulty" (*Journal of Discourses,* 19:341).

Certainly the Spirit speaks, among other things, of the ability to recognize the evil that surrounds us and the power to prevail against it. As recipients of the Spirit's influence, we, like Joseph of old, will flee temptation and see it for the danger it truly is. President George Q. Cannon said, "If we call upon [God] in faith to bless us and seek to enjoy the companionship of the Holy Spirit so ordering our lives that God can, consistently, bless us and the Spirit of the Lord can abide with us, we receive strength to overcome every evil and our minds instinctively recoil from the commission of any act which might grieve that Spirit or bring a stain upon our own character or upon the divine cause in which we are engaged" (*Truth,* 1:343–44).

The continuing influence of the Holy Ghost develops within us a spiritual intuition of sorts. We learn to distinguish more accurately between good and evil and spontaneously reject those things that are not of God. Righteous choices become second nature, and our increased spiritual sensitivity sounds the alarm when sin is near, causing us to automatically pull back from anything that offends the Spirit and weakens our relationship with him. If our relationship with the Holy Ghost is strong, anything contrary to his voice will be offensive—even repulsive—to us, never attractive or inviting. Out of sheer discomfort, we will avoid those things that are not of God, seeking only for the peaceful feeling that comes when the Holy Ghost is present. That is why King Lamoni, his wife, and his servants, after experiencing conversion through the testimony of Ammon, "had no more desire to do evil" (Alma 19:33). Their hearts were pure, they were filled with the Spirit, and their only desire was righteousness.

Those who live in the influence of the Spirit experience a process of spiritual maturation, unlike those who do not allow the Holy Ghost to fully manifest himself in their lives. Never has this been as apparent to me as it was during the time we spent in the mission field. One day each month, we received a group of new missionaries from the Missionary Training Center. We loved them from the first minute we met them. They were always excited and ready to convert the world (or at least the entire city of Boston). Almost without exception, they were enthusiastic, a little timid, slightly nervous, and *always* tired. In their eyes we saw goodness and purity and great personal expectations about the missionary each wanted to become. They spent time with us that evening at the mission home, where we became better acquainted over dinner and during a testimony meeting. The next morning they left the Belmont Chapel with their first companions. We said good-bye and knew, from that moment on, they would be forever changed.

The following day each month we saw the results of serving the Lord faithfully when the departing missionaries came to the mission home for one last evening together. There was joy in their eyes and confidence in their step. They were still tired but full of the satisfaction that comes from wearing out one's life in the service of God. These missionaries were seasoned, happy, excited, strong, dedicated, and pure. As wonderful as they were the day they arrived in our mission, they were even more wonderful by the time they left us to return home. How we loved them. Our final evening together was always full of tears and laughter as we remembered the incredible experiences of their missions. What a joy it was to hear their testimonies, which had been nurtured and tested, forged and strengthened through the blessings—and challenges—of the service they had rendered. These missionaries had given themselves to the Lord as they walked the streets of Massachusetts, day in and day out. The Lord, in return, had blessed them with manifestations of the Spirit, which had transformed them into men and women of great strength and deep faith.

As we watched these two different groups of missionaries—those arriving and those returning home—it was interesting to see the contrast between them. The spiritual growth that took place between the day they came to us as new missionaries and the day their missions ended could not have been more profound, nor could it have been duplicated under any other circumstance. It was phenomenal. Having witnessed the entire process (for most of them) from beginning to end, we were truly amazed. Many things had shaped them during this time: experiences, companions, ward members, responsibility, hard work. But the one thing that had truly *changed* them was the Holy Ghost. The Spirit had purified them. It had taught and testified to them. It had strengthened their testimonies and given them courage and power to testify to others. It had evidenced itself in their lives in a myriad of ways, all of which contributed to their growth, which was so apparent.

More than any other thing, however, it was their relationship with the Savior—through the Spirit—which had accelerated their spiritual growth in a very noticeable and profound way. Those who were the most worthy and had been the most obedient were the ones who had changed the most. Those missionaries had enjoyed the Spirit to a greater degree because of their righteousness. As they chose to keep the mission rules, live the commandments, and honor their covenants with the Lord, they became free of the confinement that disobedience brings. Their spirits could progress at a much faster rate because the Holy Ghost was able to be fully operational in their lives.

Obedience always brings spiritual growth and, with full-time missionaries, it is further accelerated by the disciplined, unselfish, and spiritually rich environment in which they live. After many months of observing these changes in our departing missionaries, we realized that their spiritual state at the end of their missions actually revealed the level of their obedience during the time they had served. The spiritual maturity they acquired was an extremely reliable indicator to how much they had given to the Lord and willingly sacrificed in order to be absolutely faithful and obedient.

My husband and I now use this "system" on our own returned-missionary sons to discover what kind of missionaries they have been. All we have to do is look closely at the change they have experienced. If it is a great, or as Alma called it, a "mighty change" (Alma 5:14), we know that their obedience—and their relationship with the Savior and the Holy Ghost—have been mighty, as well.

The connection between obedience and spiritual maturity is as certain as the connection between sin and sorrow. It is effective in the lives of each of Heavenly Father's children; all who follow Him will reap blessings. Similar to the law of the harvest, this law requires obedience in return for spiritual growth. It is as impossible to grow spiritually while sinning as it is to decrease in spirituality while living a righteous life. It simply cannot happen. Expecting different results would be like planting corn and hoping to harvest tomatoes. No matter how badly you want tomatoes, no matter how long you pray for them or persuade the plants to be tomatoes, it is simply not going to happen. There is not even the slightest chance you will get anything but corn. We reap what we sow, and the growth of our spirits comes one way and one way only: through obedience to the commandments of God.

When we obey God, we use our agency to lay down our own desires in pursuit of his will. Yielding to the will of God brings the Spirit into our lives to an even greater degree. Through this submission, a process occurs similar to that of strengthening a muscle. When a muscle becomes submissive—for example, when it is pressing upon a heavy weight—it may seem at one point to be in a position of weakness. Not so. As the muscle works and then recovers, it gains greater strength than it had before the whole process began. Much like this muscle, our spirits, when submitted to God, may also seem initially to be in a position of weakness. This, also, is not so. In reality, that submission brings a power and a strength much greater than we originally possessed. In this way, obedience brings an increase in spiritual maturity. Just as a well-developed muscle is proof that it has been exercised, spiritual growth is a certain indication of a righteous—and spiritually submissive—life.

Spiritual maturity is evidenced in many ways, some of which are not seen, and some of which are. The spiritually mature *person*, however, is easily recognizable. Knowledge and testimony are personal and deep, never showy and never used to intimidate or manipulate. An understanding of self is accompanied by a quiet confidence that comes from knowing who they are in the eyes of the Lord. Humility is interwoven in all they do, for it is a part of their being. Righteousness becomes a reflex, and faith permeates every facet of life. A personal relationship with the Savior is apparent, and his attributes shine forth through the eyes of the spiritually mature. There is deep peacefulness in the countenance of those who walk by the light of the Spirit. These and many other characteristics easily identify those whose lives are led by God through his intermediary, the Holy Ghost.

The Holy Ghost further reveals himself in our lives as he strengthens our relationships with others. Strong bonds of love and unity are formed when he is present. This happens between family members, friends, or even just acquaintances. Sharing experiences with the Spirit creates enduring friendships between those who are present, even though it may be the only experience two people may share in this lifetime. Those of us who enjoy membership in The Church of Jesus Christ of Latter-day Saints recognize a deep connection we have with others in the Church; we are bound together in a very unique way. Because we have experiences with each other as well as with the Spirit, we develop a love and kinship that comes through the sharing of the heart, which is the Spirit's most effective tool. As we partake of the sacrament, fast, attend the temple, participate in baptisms, pray, and serve in the Church together, we form spiritual ties with each other, and enduring attachments result. No matter where we go in the Church, we feel an immediate friendship with one other. Elder James M. Paramore reminded us of this feeling, which has always existed among the followers of Christ:

"The Apostle Paul, himself a convert to Christ and His truths, personally learned not only of the great eternal truths which edified his whole being and changed his life, but also that he belonged to the body of Christ—the people of the kingdom of God on earth who loved and served each other with an open heart and spirit because of the love they felt. Listen to his words as he described how it was: 'Now therefore ye are no more strangers and foreigners, but fellowcitizens with the saints, and of the household of God' (Eph. 2:19)" ("Gospel," 28).

During my husband's professional baseball career, there

were many occasions when a member of the Church in the back of a crowd of autograph-seekers would call out, "Brother Murphy!" That always got Dale's attention and brought an instant connection. More than once, Dale was good-naturedly accused by his teammates of dropping an easy fly ball or making a bad throw to help a player on the opposing team who just happened to be a member of the Church. They loved to kid him about that.

But truly, the connection between all of us is a reality. Have you ever felt the relief of locating a ward in a foreign country or noticing someone in your office reading a Book of Mormon? When we find each other, we feel an undeniable bond, and we become immediate friends. Of all the things we are known for in the Church, perhaps this is one of the most complimentary: the brotherhood and sisterhood that exists among us. Most of us know it is there, but we may not realize why. Certainly we feel immediate trust; we understand one another's goals; we share similar values. Living the gospel should make us more patient, less judgmental, and generally happier, all of which make us better people and better friends. But one factor, often overlooked, that contributes greatly in building this bond between us is the effect of the Holy Ghost and the moments we share together—with him. The Spirit's ability to melt hearts together is truly one of the greatest blessings we enjoy in mortality.

The Holy Ghost is a purifying force in our lives. He is a sanctifier. If we will but lean on his wisdom and follow his instructions, we will become pure and worthy instruments to be used by the Lord as he sees fit. We are the Lord's servants, who have been sent to do his work. It therefore stands to reason that only a messenger sent directly by him could properly guide us on his behalf. Because he is counting on us, he does not leave us without a way to receive his counsel, instruction, guidance, and love.

Throughout our days of mortality, we will never know a better friend, never rely on a more dependable guide, and never walk with a more exalting companion than the Holy Ghost. We will never feel with greater conviction or see with more certain vision than we will feel or see those things of which he testifies. He can bring peace, instill truth, impart blessings, and inspire testimony as no other source is qualified or able to do. He can establish the reality of moments past as if we had been physically present and fill our souls with the same joy that would have been ours had we been there ourselves. Elder S. Dilworth Young spoke of this ability when he said:

"By the Spirit of the Holy Ghost . . . I can bridge the nineteen hundred odd years between our day and the time of our beloved Lord. By that Spirit I can go with him as he walked the hills of Judea; I can follow him to the cross; I can hear the discussion at Emmaus and can enjoy the perfect love for him which his disciples felt after his resurrection . . . While the distance in time through the years has been long, it seems but a short time because of this Spirit" (Conference Report, Apr. 1953, 87).

Beloved King Benjamin was instructed by an angel to teach his people the plan of salvation. Still today, we learn from his wisdom and diligently heed his warnings, for there are some things, namely the things of God, that never change. In Mosiah 2:36 he gives us great insight as to what happens when we follow the guidance of the Holy Ghost. He tells us, "The Spirit of the Lord . . . [will] guide you in wisdom's paths that ye may be *blessed, prospered, and preserved*" (emphasis added). Consider the significance of that all-encompassing promise. Is there any limit to the many ways the Holy Ghost will bless us?

The Spirit touches every part of our lives. The Spirit is willing to direct every facet of our lives and use his influence to shape us into godlike beings. He performs tasks so essential to our exaltation that, without him, we could never fulfill the true measure of our creation. Although the world may know the name of the Holy Ghost, they are virtually oblivious to the reality of who he is and the mission he performs. How fortunate we are to know the value of the gift given us by our Father in Heaven and to understand how much we need it.

Elder Marion G. Romney said, "You can make every decision in your life correctly if you can learn to follow the guidance of the Holy Spirit" (Conference Report, Oct. 1961, 60). Stop and think for a moment about what that means. Is it stated so simply that we miss the magnificence of this promise? Following the promptings of the Holy Ghost will help us to make not some but *every* decision correctly. Following his voice will lead us—gradually yet absolutely—to the perfection we all seek.

STEP SEVEN

Identify promptings that come to you which require action on your part, and record them in your scripture journal. As you complete each action you were inspired to take, circle the prompting you wrote down. For example, you may feel inspired to check on an elderly neighbor. Write it down and then circle it after the visit has been made.

From the scripture journal of Nephi, grandson of Helaman:

And they did pray for that which they most desired; and they desired that the Holy Ghost should be given unto them.

—3 NEPHI 19:9

CHAPTER EIGHT

IS IT THE HOLY GHOST SPEAKING?

*It has thus been revealed unto me, . . . by the
manifestation of the Spirit of God.*
ALMA 5:47

The prophet Abraham was commanded to sacrifice his only son and heir to his promised covenants. The scriptures record that "God . . . said unto him" (Genesis 22:1), leaving no doubt in Abraham's mind who had spoken. As he walked up the mountain to face what appeared to be his destiny, he knew his course was set, for his faith was strong and his obedience certain. We do not know exactly what passed through his mind as he and Isaac first set out to perform the heart-wrenching task. We can, however, be certain that Abraham knew it was God himself who had given the command.

Moses saw the Lord "in a flame of fire in the midst of a bush" and there was issued the call of his life: to "bring forth [God's] people the children of Israel out of Egypt" (Exodus

3:10). He had no doubt that this direction came from God, for he had seen him with his own eyes. As he walked out of Egypt, the children of Israel close behind, he knew he was truly on God's errand. Like the parted waters of the Red Sea, the Lord would protect them. Like manna from heaven, he would sustain them. Moses did not fear, for the Lord was with them. God had commanded him, and he knew it was by the Lord they were led.

How could the prophet Nephi be absolutely sure he should build a ship, load it with his family and their possessions, and set sail upon uncharted waters for a place they couldn't see and didn't know for certain even existed? Was he frightened in the least as he climbed aboard? As they set out to sea and watched the land disappear in the distance, did he, for even one moment, wonder if this truly was the will of the Lord or was it, instead, some kind of misinterpreted manifestation? No. Nephi did not doubt or hesitate to obey. The voice of the Lord had come to him (1 Nephi 17:7–8) and personally given the instructions. He knew he need not fear, for God truly had spoken and he would be with them.

How do *we* know for certain when the Lord has spoken? Usually he does not speak to us as he spoke to Abraham or Moses. His voice usually comes so softly that we must train ourselves to hear it, for only those who hear it can recognize it as his and will thus be able to respond to its promptings. As Elizabeth Barrett Browning wrote:

Earth's crammed with heaven,
And every common bush afire with God;
And only he who sees takes off his shoes.
                    (in Bartlett, Quotations, *431)*

There are many sacred moments in our lives when the Holy Ghost attempts to communicate with us. We can only understand the true significance of those moments if we know how to recognize and respond to the Spirit's voice.

Have you ever become frustrated waiting for an answer to your prayers, straining your spiritual ears to hear, and watching for any hint of a response? Do answers that require patience (as most do) cause you to wonder if your prayers have even been heard at all? A Primary song expresses well the questions we all ask from time to time and then gives the tender and reassuring answer:

Heavenly Father, are you really there?
And do you hear and answer ev'ry child's prayer?
. . . .
Pray, he is there;
Speak, he is list'ning.
                    (Perry, "Child's Prayer," Songbook,
                    12; used by permission)

Elder Boyd K. Packer taught: "Sometimes you may struggle with a problem and not get an answer. What could be wrong? It may be that you are not doing anything wrong.

"It may be that you have not done the right things long enough. Remember, you cannot force spiritual things.

"Sometimes we are confused simply because we won't take no for an answer. . . .

"Put difficult questions in the back of your minds and go about your lives. Ponder and pray quietly and consistently about them.

"The answer may not come as a lightning bolt. It may come as a little inspiration here and a little there, 'line upon line, precept upon precept' (D&C 98:12)" ("Prayers," 21).

Truly, it is an exercise of faith to remain steady and sure as we wait upon the Lord's inspiration. By demonstrating patience we express our deep desire for divine assistance.

Elder Dallin Oaks explained: "The Lord will speak to us through the Spirit in his own time and in his own way. Many people do not understand this principle. They believe that when they are ready and when it suits their convenience, they can call upon the Lord and he will immediately respond, even in the precise way they have prescribed. Revelation does not come that way. . . .

"The principle stated in [D&C 88:68] applies to every communication from our Heavenly Father: 'It shall be in his own time, and in his own way, and according to his own will.'" ("Teaching," 10–11). In the matter of answers to prayer, patience truly is a virtue.

There are many reasons why we often hesitate to accept answers from the Lord once they are given. We may question inspiration simply because we doubt our own ability to receive or interpret it correctly. We may resist answers if they are not those we wanted or are willing to accept. Sometimes we rationalize away sacred instruction simply because we do not want to put forth the necessary effort to respond in the way that was directed. We may also fail to acknowledge that we have received an answer to our prayers when the Lord is requiring things of us that are unpleasant or difficult. No matter the reason, anything that keeps us from recognizing and following the Holy Ghost creates detours that lead us away from our Father in Heaven.

Most of us have probably, at one time or another, wished that if only we could see a vision, if only we could hear the voice of God telling us what to do, if only we had absolute proof that our answers were from him, then we would do *whatever* he asked of us—no question. What we may not realize is that the Holy Ghost has been bestowed upon us for that very purpose—to provide us with the knowledge, understanding, assurance, and peace that only God himself can give. Receiving a manifestation of the Spirit is no less an answer than seeing an angel by your bedside or hearing a voice from the heavens. The Holy Ghost brings convincing power to all who are in tune with the Lord and receptive to his will. We may never receive a visitation or actually hear words spoken by a heavenly messenger, but we do not need such manifestations to know with certainty that the Lord is speaking when we hear him through the voice of the Holy Ghost.

Are we confident enough in our ability to recognize the Spirit's voice that we obey without hesitation? Do we know, as surely as did Abraham or Moses or Nephi, when we have actually heard the Lord speaking through the promptings of the Spirit? Or does doubt tempt us to turn back as we climb our spiritual mountains or board the ship to our own personal promised land? How can we be certain, as they were, that it truly is God who has spoken?

My almost-teenaged daughter came to me one day feeling uncomfortable about a snowboarding trip she was about to take. She couldn't exactly put her finger on it, but she was nervous and didn't know why. Was it just anxiety, or was it, in fact, a voice of warning from the Holy Ghost? She wanted to know. Certainly a burning bush would have come in handy at that moment, but there I was, trying to explain impressions that may be difficult, at any age, to fully understand. How can we know if what we hear is truly the voice of the Spirit? Is it possible to mistake our own desires or fears for inspiration from the Holy Ghost? What is the best way to identify the voice we hear?

Thankfully, my young daughter seemed relieved after my heartfelt but somewhat inadequate attempt to teach her how to recognize the Spirit in her life. She left on her trip, cell phone in hand (in case she needed to call me for further reassurance), and returned that evening with a smile on her face, the uneasiness of the morning long forgotten. During the time she was making her way up and down the mountain that day, however, I was at home, rehearsing in my mind all the things I *should* have said to her. I should have told her to pray for the power of discernment to be able to differentiate between the promptings of the Holy Ghost and our own emotions. I might have suggested she ask for a priesthood blessing to clear her mind and point her toward things that were truly of the Spirit. I could have taught her that genuine inspiration tugs at our hearts and our minds and struggles to get our attention over and over again, if we are humbly and truly seeking it. Unless our hearts become hardened or pride keeps us from listening, the Spirit will continue to tap on our shoulder.

Ofttimes, the mere longevity of a thought is an indication that it is the Holy Ghost speaking. I remembered the time years ago when my husband and I received a strong impression that we should move our family from Georgia to Utah. Atlanta had been our home for fifteen wonderful years, and the thought of leaving seemed incomprehensible. As we were trying to understand the promptings we were receiving, we experienced for ourselves the persistent nature of the Spirit. Every morning, we would wake up and say, "What in the world are we thinking? We can't leave Atlanta. We love Atlanta. Our lives are here. We are staying!" But as the day wore on and the Spirit's gentle influence seeped into our hearts, we gradually changed our minds. By the time we went to bed, we would look at each other and say, "We are moving. We hear the Spirit speaking. Let's start packing!" By the next morning, it was as if sleep had erased from our minds the conviction of the night before, and we were back to "What in the world are we thinking?" The Spirit would do his work again day after day, and by bedtime every night, we would be convinced again and ready to move.

Because we are slow learners, this process continued for weeks until finally we realized that we must be testing the Spirit's patience. We knew he had been speaking to us, persuading us to listen to the Lord's will in our lives. Thankfully, he did not give up. A few months later, we packed up our young family and moved across the country. Through the years which have passed since then, we have been given an understanding of exactly why the Lord wanted us in Utah and why the Spirit just kept whispering.

As we seek the Lord's guidance, we all feel confused from time to time. It is part of the challenge of being mortal—to distinguish between our own thoughts, feelings, and emotions and the inspired directives given us by the Holy Ghost. Ironically, it is often our own confusion that keeps us from acting on the Spirit's promptings, not knowing if what we feel truly comes from God. Failure to act causes even more confusion and, before long, we are paralyzed by uncertainty and doubt.

Think about it. If you were Satan and you understood the vital role the Holy Ghost plays in our eternal progression, what would you do? Certainly you would try everything possible to keep us from hearing the Spirit's voice. You would place in front of us a world that has no concept of the mission of the Holy Ghost or the way he works in our lives. You would minimize his importance. You would take advantage of our natural-man tendency toward pride and convince us that we can make it on our own. After you had insulted the Spirit in every possible way, you would then weaken relationships with Heavenly Father and draw people into sin to close the lines of communication. Elder Robert D. Hales said, "If we are not obedient to the laws, principles, and ordinances of the gospel, the Holy Ghost will withdraw. He cannot be with us if we are angry in our hearts, contentious with our companions, or critical of the Lord's anointed. He departs whenever we are rebellious, are immoral, dress or act immodestly, are unclean or profane in mind or body, are slothful in priesthood callings and duties, or commit other sins, for 'the Spirit of the Lord doth not dwell in unholy temples'" ("Receiving," 31).

We certainly need not look far to see Satan's attempts to lure us away from our Father in Heaven. If you were Satan and wanted to disarm God's children, you would do anything possible to confuse, confound, and conflict us. The wolf does not want a shepherd among the flocks any more than Satan wants the Holy Ghost in our lives.

If Satan's attempt to quiet the Holy Ghost were to fail, the master of deceit would try the next best thing: confuse us about the source of that inspiration to stop us from acting on what we hear. Said President George Q. Cannon, "It requires the utmost care upon the part of the people who have received the Spirit of the Lord by the laying on of hands to distinguish between the voice of that Spirit and the voice of their own hearts or other spirits which may take possession of them" (*Truth,* 1:182). We must pray constantly for the spiritual perception to recognize the difference between the whisperings of the Holy Ghost and the voice that comes from any other source.

When I was just a small girl, we kept a stack of folded maps in our family's station wagon. If we were ever lost, the maps would come out, giving me immediate hope that we would eventually find our way. Nowadays, we don't even own a map, let alone carry one in our car. If we need directions, we go to the computer, enter the starting point and destination, and almost magically receive a printout of detailed instructions. Usually, these instructions are very accurate and make finding an address a painless process.

If, however, there is ever an error in the directions, you are certain to be in a noisy car driving a bunch of loud and giggly twelve-year-old girls to a volleyball tournament—which is exactly what happened to me! Evidently, the computerized instructions were not as current as the new freeway exit that we should have taken. Before long, we were hopelessly lost. This would not have been terribly unusual—people get lost every day—except that I had perfect (I thought) directions and I was following them. How could I be lost? After finally admitting it was a remote possibility, I stopped to ask for help, discovered my mistake, and drove directly to our destination.

I learned two great lessons that day that have helped me ever since. Number one: directions are only as good as the source from which you receive them. Number two: keep an extra map in your glove box—just in case.

Not unlike my dilemma that day, following inspiration

from any source other than the Holy Ghost may lead us down the wrong road. Remember, directions are only as good as their source. No matter how valiantly we follow the voice we hear, if it is not the Spirit speaking, we may find ourselves on dangerous ground. Acting on the wrong information will never lead us to the right destination. We must be cautious and alert as we determine the credibility of the source of our promptings.

To determine whether or not it is the voice of the Holy Ghost we hear, we can ask ourselves the following questions:

1. DO I FEEL THE EMOTIONS THE SPIRIT WOULD BRING?

We can know it is the Holy Ghost speaking when we feel "love, joy, peace, longsuffering, gentleness, goodness, [and] faith" (Galatians 5:22), for these are fruits, or results, of the Spirit. Mormon teaches us that meekness and lowliness of heart bring the Holy Ghost (Moroni 8:26), so when these feelings surround us, we know he is present.

After his death, Joseph Smith appeared to Brigham Young and asked him to educate the Saints concerning the feelings that accompany the Holy Ghost. He said, "They can tell the Spirit of the Lord from all other spirits; it will whisper peace and joy to their souls; it will take malice, hatred, strife and all evil from their hearts; and their whole desire will be to do good" (in Faust, "Gift," 33).

If we pay attention to the feelings that come with the inspiration we receive, we can more easily determine what is—and what is not—from the Lord. President Ezra Taft Benson deepened our understanding of this principle:

"The Holy Ghost causes our feelings to be more tender. We feel more charitable and compassionate. We are calmer. We have a greater capacity to love. People want to be around us because our very countenances radiate the influence of the Spirit. We are more godly in character. As a result, we are more sensitive to the promptings of the Holy Ghost and thus able to comprehend spiritual things" (*Come,* 20).

When acting under the Spirit's holy influence, we are more like God in every way. We think more like him; we act more like he would act. Even our emotions are tempered with celestial overtones when we live by the whisperings of the Spirit.

Because the presence of the Holy Ghost is recognized most often through our feelings, his companionship is often associated with other senses, as well. After a moving sermon, Joseph Smith said to the Saints, " When I tell you of these things which were given me by inspiration of the Holy Ghost, you are bound to receive them as sweet, and rejoice more and more" (*Teachings,* 349). How does inspiration taste sweet? The promptings of the Holy Ghost are pleasing to the senses, satisfy spiritual hunger, and leave us filled with the power of the Spirit. Alma taught that the word of God is delicious: Once it is planted in our hearts, he said, "ye will begin to say within yourselves—It must needs be that this is a good seed, or that the word is good, for it beginneth to enlarge my soul; yea, it beginneth to enlighten my understanding, yea, it beginneth to be delicious to me" (Alma 32:28.) He, too, experienced the sweetness of the word of God.

That which comes through the Holy Ghost will always reflect his nature. In contrast, "that which doth not edify is not of God" (D&C 50:23). Goodness and positive emotions are a sure indication that the Spirit is near. Anger, contention, resentment, or any other negative or destructive emotion can immediately alert us that we are not feeling impressions of the Holy Ghost. It is impossible to feel the Spirit and at the same time feel unsettled, unhappy, or afraid. We can authenticate the source of our answers by asking ourselves, "How do I feel? Is my soul at peace? Am I happy? Or do I have feelings of anxiety, unhappiness, or contempt?"

Doctrine and Covenants 11:13 names the most cherished of all feelings which come from the Spirit's presence: "Verily, verily, I say unto you, I will impart unto you of my Spirit, which shall . . . fill your soul with joy."

2. AM I WORTHY TO RECEIVE AN ANSWER?

President Joseph Fielding Smith said, "Our great duty is to so live that we may be led constantly in light and truth by this Comforter so that we may not be deceived by the many false spirits that are in the world" (*Doctrines,* 1:39). A righteous life is fundamentally essential to acquiring the companionship of the Holy Ghost, and we can more positively identify the source of our promptings by first examining our own worthiness. If our actions do not merit his guidance, we can assume he will not guide us. If we are not deserving of his counsel, it will not be given. If our spiritual strength is lacking and we have not qualified for his attending care, we can be sure he will not minister to our needs. If we have fallen into sin, we will not hear his voice. Elder Neal A. Maxwell taught, "The Holy Ghost never waits to leave until he is formally asked to leave, for his influence has already departed even as we, by our thoughts, slide towards sin" (*Family,* 86).

On the other hand, righteous choices *always* warrant promised blessings. One who holds firmly to the iron rod is entitled to the Spirit's inspired tutelage. The amount of guidance we are given will always be proportionate to the level of obedience we achieve and the degree to which we prepare ourselves to receive the light the Holy Ghost offers.

3. Is the answer in line with the living prophet?

A sure way to test inspiration that comes to us is to examine it for elements contrary to the counsel of the living prophet. He is the Lord's mouthpiece. He is our Moses and will lead us from spiritual bondage if only we will follow him. If we are out of step with the guidance of the living prophet, we are walking away from the Lord and directly toward the slavery of sin.

The First Presidency warned: "When visions, dreams, tongues, prophecy, impressions or any extraordinary gift or inspiration conveys something out of harmony with the accepted revelations of the Church or contrary to the decisions of its constituted authorities, Latter-day Saints may know that it is not of God, no matter how plausible it may appear. All faithful members are entitled to the inspiration of the Holy Spirit for themselves, their families, and for those over whom they are appointed and ordained to preside. But anything at discord with that which comes from God through the head of the Church is not to be received as authoritative or reliable" (letter, Aug. 1913, in Lee, Conference Report, Apr. 1970, 55).

Those who obtain the companionship of the Holy Ghost will also receive a testimony—through him—of the living prophet who leads us.

4. Is it within my stewardship to receive inspiration in this area?

How would you feel if a neighbor came to you with the report of a revelation he had received concerning your family? Such a thing would obviously be out of line, and it illustrates a divine principle: Each of us is entitled to personal revelation in areas over which we hold stewardship. We are not given information about who our best friend's daughter should marry, where a temple ought to be built, or when our bishop should be released. If we ever suspect the Holy Ghost has communicated such things to us, we can be absolutely certain he did not. The Spirit will never inspire us on matters over which we do not hold direct stewardship. "We should understand what can be called the principle of 'stewardship in revelation,'" said Dallin H. Oaks in 1981. "Only the president of the Church receives revelation to guide the entire Church. Only the stake president

116

receives revelation for the specific guidance of the stake. The person who receives revelation for the ward is the bishop. For a family, it is the priesthood leadership of the family. Leaders receive revelation for their own stewardships. Individuals can receive revelation to guide their own lives. But when one person purports to receive revelation for another person outside his or her own stewardship . . . you can be sure that such revelations are not from the Lord" (*Speeches*, 1:208).

Any attempt to influence a person who is outside your stewardship responsibility by claiming revelation on that person's behalf is nothing more than spiritual manipulation and is dishonest in its very nature. It is disrespectful of the sacred gift offered us by the Holy Ghost: direct communication with God on behalf of ourselves and those over whom we hold stewardship. Abusing the gift of personal revelation in this way makes a mockery of the sacred inspiration we receive and lessens the likelihood that the Spirit will speak to us at all.

5. Is it logical and reasonable?

Most often, answers from the Holy Ghost will be logical and reasonable—they will make sense. They will feel like puzzle pieces that fit together. Answers that come from the Lord will not suggest action that is nonsensical or ridiculous. For example, if I am praying to know which college to attend, and I think I have received an answer instructing me to walk to Arizona barefoot and consult my great-aunt while balancing three goldfish on my head, I can be quite sure that answer did not come from the Holy Ghost. Inspiration that comes from God is based on order—in this case, logic and reason. If this were not so, it would be impossible to follow the counsel in Doctrine and Covenants 9:8, which admonishes us to "study it out" in our minds. We must be very cautious of answers we perceive to be from the Spirit that do not fit this criterion.

There are times, however, when the Holy Ghost speaks and, at first, his promptings may *seem* illogical. Occasionally, we may be surprised at what he instructs us to do, for the Lord is truly omniscient and there are moments when we must "lean not unto [our] own understanding" (Proverbs 3:5). The senior couple who receives an answer to their prayers to serve a full-time mission, although they do not understand how it could be possible; the newly married couple who feels inspired to take a job far from family members and friends but sees no reason to do so; the tenth-grader who feels prompted to sit at a different table for lunch and, although wondering why, does so and ends up sharing the gospel with someone he barely knows—each of these is an example of times it seems the Lord's direction, for one reason or another, does not make sense.

If at first a prompting seems illogical, and we are not certain it is from the Holy Ghost, we must remember the Lord's will in our lives is not always what we imagine it to be. He may ask things of us that seem difficult—even impossible. But think of those who considered it illogical to build an ark to be saved from a catastrophic flood, or the Israelites who thought it impossible to cross the Red Sea on foot. What at first appeared wrong eventually proved right because God sees with a clear vision, and we are not always capable of such clarity. He knows eternity, whereas our understanding is severely limited by the simple fact that we are mortal. Because of the Lord's incomparable wisdom, no answer sent through the Holy Ghost will ever be wrong. Once we know it is the Spirit speaking, we must follow the inspiration we are given.

When we receive answers that seem illogical, unreasonable, or impossible, how do we distinguish whether their source truly is the Holy Ghost? Until we know for sure, we cannot act, for we do not yet know it is God who has spoken. We must test the source of our answers by determining if the prompting was accompanied by the feelings of the Spirit. We must think through the results of the action the prompting inspired and discern whether it is something the Lord would truly require of us. We must set aside our own selfishness and pride, sincerely desiring God's will in our lives.

To be sure, we cannot judge communication from the Spirit based solely on logic; we must seek to understand the Lord's purposes and gain a confirmation of his will. Once we know for sure, we must act on the inspiration given. Whether we act on answers not of God or fail to act on those which are, either way we have misread the communications of the Spirit. If we make this kind of a mistake, where will we be? Perhaps standing by the ark in the pouring rain or waiting on the shores of the Red Sea.

6. Do I Have an Open Heart?

The scriptures are filled with references to the heart. We are told that "the Lord looketh on the heart" (1 Samuel 16:7). We are counseled to "seek him with all thy heart and with all thy soul" (Deuteronomy 4:29) and "love the Lord thy God with all thine heart" (Deuteronomy 6:5). The righteous are identified as those having "clean hands, and a pure heart" (Psalm 24:4) and the rebellious as those who have "hardened their heart" (John 12:40). We are admonished to experience a "mighty change in your hearts" (Alma 5:14) and, ultimately, to become bound with charity to those around us—to be "of one heart" (Moses 7:18).

What does it mean to have an open heart? The definition of "open heart" mirrors that of "honest in heart," as explained by Elder Marvin J. Ashton: "What does it mean to be honest in heart? It describes an individual who is open to truth, who will evaluate information or people without prejudice" ("Measure," 15).

A person who has an open heart is full of faith and free from pride and unrighteous judgment. An open heart demonstrates complete trust in and devotion to the Lord as well as a willingness to accept any answer, which is itself an indication that the person who asks has the faith necessary to obey the promptings given. Having an open heart is a condition of the soul that invites the Holy Ghost to speak unabated and operate unrestrained.

Why must we have an open heart? To hear the will of the Lord, we must open ourselves up to any possibility, be ready to accept any answer, for then our spirits, through humility, are willing to conform to the Lord's desires for our lives. If our heart is closed in any way or to any degree, the Lord cannot freely bless us with answers we seek.

To know if we have an open heart, we can ask ourselves, Am I prepared to accept the Lord's will? Am I willing to act on the answer the Lord may give, despite any disappointment I might feel or any disagreement I might have with the promptings that come? Have I turned my life over to him with complete submissiveness and surrender? Are my personal desires the true issue or is the will of the Lord my greatest desire? Answering these questions can help us see clearly whether or not we possess an open heart.

Elder Boyd K. Packer taught: "It is not wise to wrestle with the revelations with such insistence as to demand immediate answers or blessings to your liking.

"You cannot force spiritual things. Such words as *compel, coerce, constrain, pressure, demand* do not describe our privileges with the Spirit.

"You can no more force the Spirit to respond than you can force a bean to sprout, or an egg to hatch before its time. You can create a climate to foster growth; . . . but you cannot force or compel. . . .

"Do not be impatient to gain great spiritual knowledge. Let

it grow, help it grow; but do not force it, or you will open the way to be misled" (*Edified,* 337–38).

When we possess a heart open to the Lord's will, we do not attempt to pressure answers from him. If our primary motive is to simply get our own way, we close off our hearts as well as the avenue in which the Holy Ghost must travel.

7. Have I used the Lord's formula recorded in Doctrine and Covenants 9?

We are familiar with the instructions found in Doctrine and Covenants 9:8–9 that direct us to "study it out in your mind; then you must ask me if it be right, and if it is right I will cause that your bosom shall burn within you; therefore, you shall feel that it is right. But if it be not right you shall have no such feelings, but you shall have a stupor of thought that shall cause you to forget the thing which is wrong."

We must use a combination of mind and heart to identify our answers and recognize their source. A correct answer is accompanied by a feeling within, often referred to as a burning in the bosom. President Boyd K. Packer explained that such a burning "is not purely a physical sensation. It is more like a warm light shining within your being" ("Personal," 60).

The scriptures are given to instruct us. Doctrine and Covenants 9:9 clearly teaches how to receive answers and know for certain their source. Is it not reasonable that those who truly seek the Lord will give heed to these inspired words?

8. AM I WAITING FOR THE "SPECTACULAR"?

Many times we overlook answers from the Lord, thinking they will come in grand fashion, something more magnificent than a quiet, simple feeling. At these times we are in danger of being deceived or even missing the answers to our prayers altogether. Elder Dallin H. Oaks explained: "Some [people] have looked exclusively for the great manifestations that are recorded in the scriptures and have failed to recognize the still, small voice that is given to them. . . .

"We need to know that the Lord rarely speaks loudly. His messages almost always come in a whisper. . . .

"Not understanding these principles of revelation, some people postpone acknowledging their testimony until they have experienced a miraculous event" ("Teaching," 11–12, 14).

How many of us keep praying for the same thing, unaware that our answer has already come? Surely no one believes that an answer to prayer will come with a display of fireworks or a lightning bolt or some other heavenly manifestation. Yet we often use those terms to describe an unknown but dramatic occurrence we suppose should accompany answers that come from God. Perhaps that is because we live in a world dominated by media that dwells on the spectacular and a movie industry that thrives on special effects to which we are constantly exposed. Perhaps we want something magnificent, thinking it to be a true indication that it comes from God. Or perhaps we simply desire experiences like those of the ancient prophets that fill the pages of our scriptures.

No matter the reason, we must never overlook the great privilege that is ours to walk daily with a member of the Godhead, the Holy Ghost. We must watch for promptings in the quiet moments of our day, remembering that those are the most likely times the Spirit will whisper in our ear. There is a reason the Holy Ghost is known as the still, small voice. It is because he speaks in a still, small way.

We can know for certain when the Lord speaks to us, for the Holy Ghost will impress his words deep in our hearts. The Holy Ghost is a loyal and devoted friend. His divine mission is to guide us, and he will stand ever faithful to that cause. He will reveal himself to us as we carefully watch for him, and he will direct our paths as we consistently follow his voice.

STEP EIGHT

Think back to a time you prayed for something specific. Rather than focusing on what it was you desired, however, think about the answer to your prayer. If you received an answer, how did you know it was from God? Record your thoughts in your scripture journal.

If you weren't sure you received an answer or if you were uncertain the answer truly came from God, think back over what you have just read in this chapter. With those things in mind, ask yourself if you did, perhaps, receive an answer after all. Now that you understand how to discern heavenly answers to prayers, you are equipped to hear the Spirit's whisperings. Ponder this and record your feelings in your scripture journal.

From the scripture journal of the apostle John:

He that hath an ear, let him hear what the Spirit saith.
—REVELATION 2:11

CHAPTER NINE

WE MUST RESPOND

Do according to . . . the directions of the Spirit.
DOCTRINE AND COVENANTS 62:8

A man I know (we'll call him David) had a good friend (we'll call him Tom) who lived in a faraway city. They both led busy lives and did not speak to each other often. But every once in a while, and always when David was experiencing a trial in his life, the phone would ring, and Tom would be on the other end. Without even saying hello, Tom would immediately say, "David, why am I calling you?" When prompted by the Spirit, Tom never hesitated to act—he simply picked up the phone and dialed David's number. No excuses, no delays. He heard the Spirit's whisper, felt his guiding hand, and instantly responded.

The prophet Nephi, upon returning to Jerusalem to obtain the brass plates, "was led by the Spirit, not knowing beforehand the things which [he] should do" (1 Nephi 4:6). Although uncertain about what he might encounter as he approached the house of Laban, he had no uncertainty that the Holy Ghost would prompt him to the course of action he must follow. Once the Spirit spoke, Nephi listened and obeyed.

President Thomas S. Monson has taught, "Never postpone a prompting of the Spirit" (*Inspiring,* 18). Experience has taught him that failing to act when moved upon by the Holy Ghost not only brings regret but causes opportunities to be forever lost. On the other hand, immediately responding to the Spirit's voice always brings joy. Clearly, that is the better choice.

What do *we* do when we hear the Spirit speaking? Do we stop, consider for a moment, wonder if we are actually hearing the Holy Ghost, and then go about our lives as if the prompting had never come at all? Or do we incline our spiritual ear, pay attention to his voice, and act on his direction? When the Spirit speaks to us, do *we* know what to do?

President Lorenzo Snow taught, "Now, if we really desire to draw near to God . . . if we wish to establish within ourselves that faith which we read about and by which ancient Saints performed such wonderful works, we must, after we obtain the Holy Spirit, hearken to its whisperings and conform to its suggestions, and by no act of our lives drive it from us" (*Journal of Discourses,* 23:192).

Just as "faith without works is dead" (James 2:20), when the promptings of the Spirit are not followed by action, the will of God is frustrated and our spiritual progression is seriously delayed. If we do not take steps along the path designated by the Spirit, how will we hope to arrive at the destination to which he guides us? Knowing it is his voice we hear, why would we not immediately obey? Nothing should deter us, for our ultimate goal of exaltation hangs in the balance.

Each of us must look inward and identify what may keep us from immediately obeying the promptings of the Spirit. If we understand why we do what we do, we can then begin to change. Are we unsure of how to react when he speaks? Do we feel uncomfortable responding? Are we afraid, at times, of what others may think? Is there something we are avoiding because it requires more effort than we are willing to put forth? President Joseph F. Smith instructed, "Let us do whatsoever that Spirit directs without fear of the consequences" (*Doctrine*, 59).

Certainly, nothing can be worth putting aside the Spirit's direction. No matter our reasons, anything that keeps us from responding to his still, small voice has no place in us. Such things stand in our way of fully realizing our relationship with the Holy Ghost and deeply affect the way he operates in our lives.

Each time we brush against the veil and experience a moment of communion with the Spirit, we have the opportunity to be changed. Obeying promptings changes us for the better; ignoring them moves us further away from God. Every bit of inspiration, if followed, gives us opportunities to progress. Our progression depends upon our ability to move forward, which is only possible if we are willing to move our feet. The Holy Ghost will tell us what to do; we need only have the courage to respond to his suggestions. If we do not, it is as if we are sitting in a cold, dark room, leaning against a door marked "Exit." If only we would turn around, read the word, recognize what it means, open the door, and walk out into the warm, bright sunlight, we would wonder whatever delayed such an action in the first place. It is so easy to turn the knob and open the door to the Spirit's influence, but to do so, we must resist the urge to sit still and delay our response. We must act.

The Lord gives us the direction of the Holy Ghost to ease our way through mortality and has thus provided a way that we may escape, as much as possible, unnecessary bumps along the way. Listening alone will not do; we must take each prompting and put it into action. How foolish it would be to spend a lifetime living worthy of the Spirit's guidance, train our ears to hear his voice, wait for and receive his inspiration, and then not act upon what we are given. Such an idea is not just illogical; it defeats the very purpose of striving for the Spirit in the first place. Who would complete all but the last day of a college semester and then pack up and go home? That is exactly what we do when we fail to act—which is the last necessary step in living by the whisperings of the Spirit.

The remodeling of our spiritual selves takes place as we respond over time to the inspiration of the Holy Ghost. Consider this thought by C. S. Lewis: "Imagine yourself as a living house. God comes in to rebuild that house. At first, perhaps, you can understand what He is doing. He is getting the drains right and stopping the leaks in the roof and so on: you knew that those jobs needed doing and so you were not surprised. But presently he starts knocking the house about in a way that hurts abominably and does not seem to make sense. What on earth is He up to? The explanation is that He is building quite a different house from the one you thought of—throwing out a new wing here, putting on an extra floor there, running up towers, making courtyards. You thought you were going to be made into a decent little cottage but He is building a palace. He intends to come and live in it Himself" (*Christianity*, 160). Each time we listen and act on the direction of the Holy Ghost, we become a little less of a cottage and a little more of a palace; each time we follow his direction, we become a little more like God.

Nephi, through his example, teaches us much about responding to spiritual promptings in our lives. He and his brothers, on an errand from the Lord, returned to Jerusalem to obtain the brass plates from Laban, a powerful and wicked man. This was not an easy task, yet the spiritual survival of their posterity depended on their success, for without this written record they would certainly forget the Lord. Motivated by extraordinary faith, Nephi entered the city, unaware of what was ahead and yet certain the Spirit would direct him. He saw Laban drunk in the street, and suddenly the Holy Ghost spoke. The scriptures record the exchange as the Spirit directed Nephi three times to kill Laban in order to obtain the plates. After the third time Nephi finally admitted the reason for his failing to respond: "I said in my heart: Never at any time have I shed the blood of man. And I shrunk and would that I might not slay him" (1 Nephi 4:10). Instinctively, Nephi hoped there would be another way, but as he considered the situation, he understood exactly what had to be done and why. We glimpse his thoughts as we read the verses following, learning how we, too, can be motivated to act on the promptings we receive, even those that direct us to take a difficult action.

First, Nephi "*remembered* the words of the Lord which he spake unto [him] in the wilderness, saying that: Inasmuch as thy seed shall keep my commandments, they shall prosper in the land" (1 Nephi 4:14; emphasis added). Next, Nephi *thought* about the words of the Lord and realized that "they could not keep the commandments of the Lord . . . save they should have the law" (1 Nephi 4:15). Without the scriptures—the brass plates—it would be not just unlikely but impossible for any succeeding generation to live in righteousness. The effects of living without God's word would be devastating. At this point, Nephi was given an understanding of the Spirit's direction that only moments before had appeared unthinkable. Nephi *knew* why Laban had been delivered into his hands: "that [he] might obtain the records" (1 Nephi 4:17). Despite his initial reaction, Nephi "*did obey* the voice of the Spirit, and . . . smote off [Laban's] head with his own sword" (1 Nephi 4:18; emphasis added).

As we apply this scripture to our own lives, we see four

things we can do as we, like Nephi, respond to inspiration when it comes:

1. We must *remember* the things the Lord has told us in the past—through the words of others, the scriptures, and our own personal revelation. As we reflect on those things, we will receive a greater understanding of what the Lord would have us do today.

2. We must *think* about what the Spirit is saying and how it relates to what we have already been taught.

3. We will then *know* why we have been inspired as we have. We will see the Lord's purposes more clearly and have a greater understanding of the direction we have been given.

4. We will then have the confidence to *obey* the Spirit's promptings. The Holy Ghost will witness to us that the inspiration truly comes from God.

If we follow this pattern in our own lives—to remember, to think, to know, and to obey—we, too, can be led by the Spirit. Like Nephi, we will make decisions based on logic of the mind as well as the inspiration of the heart.

The Lord himself taught the importance of doing just that: using our minds and our hearts to interpret the promptings of the Holy Ghost. The scriptures are filled with such counsel. Mosiah 7:33 speaks of "turn[ing] to the Lord with full purpose of heart, . . . with all diligence of mind," and 1 Chronicles 28:9 admonishes us to "serve him [God] with a perfect heart and with a willing mind." The Lord explained to Oliver Cowdery what is involved in the "spirit of revelation" (D&C 8:3). He said, "I will tell you in your mind and in your heart, by the Holy Ghost" (v. 2). Again speaking to Oliver, the Lord said, "Cast your mind upon the night that you cried unto me in your heart. . . . Did I not speak peace to your mind . . . ?" (D&C 6:22–23). The city of Enoch was called Zion by the Lord because its people were "of one heart and one mind" (Moses 7:18), evidently the crowning, perfecting, and qualifying state that made it possible for them to be "taken up into heaven" to dwell with God (Moses 7:21).

King Benjamin, beloved by his people, stood at the temple and taught them one last time before his death. As he began, he admonished them to use every way available to understand what he was about to say: "You should hearken unto me, and open your ears that ye may hear, and your hearts that ye may understand, and your minds that the mysteries of God may be unfolded to your view" (Mosiah 2:9). By heavenly design, the combination of both heart and mind brings an understanding of things spoken by the Spirit. Clearly, our Father in Heaven requires all the energy of our souls in return for sought-after answers and spiritual insights that only the Holy Ghost can give.

We cannot respond properly to the Lord using only our heart or only our mind. The prophet Abinadi stood bravely in King Noah's court, his life in peril, yet he was undeterred by any fear. As he bore fervent testimony of Christ and his gospel, he boldly called the wicked to repentance. He accused the false priests of "pretend[ing]" to teach truth and leading the people astray (Mosiah 12:25). He told them they had not "applied [their] hearts to understanding" and by failing to do so, had "not been wise" (Mosiah 12:27). Through his words, we see the result for those who do not use their hearts as well as their minds to understand the workings of the Spirit. They see only facts, not the reason behind them; only rules, not the spirit by which they are given. Using only a mind and not a heart creates a strictly temporal perspective based on quantifiables, whereas a spiritual understanding focuses on the tender communications of the Holy Ghost.

The importance of the heart in such matters is illustrated by author Antoine de Saint-Exupery in his classic work, *The Little Prince:* "And now here is my secret, a very simple secret: It is only with the heart that one can see rightly; what is essential is invisible to the eye" (70). Similarly, relying on the emotions of the heart alone would create an incomplete picture and give us only a portion of necessary insights—for it is through the mind we are able to find logic, understanding, and reason in the promptings we receive. We need both the heart and the mind to truly understand the communications of the Spirit.

Once we understand the whisperings of the Holy Ghost, we must then allow them to make a difference in our lives. We must go and do, knowing the Lord's guidance cannot have an effect if we do not follow it. Whether we fail to act when inspired or never hear the Spirit in the first place, the results are practically the same. Resisting the Spirit's promptings leaves us in the same predicament as if the gift of the Holy Ghost had never been given at all. We have all been without him for some portion of our lives, even those baptized at the age of eight. But those who have received the Holy Ghost and then, for some reason, lost him, understand to a greater degree the sorrow we all would feel were he permanently unavailable to us. Without him, we would be alone in the world, living without truth and testimony. Repentance, progression, and perfection would be impossible to achieve and we, as many before have done, would "dwindle in unbelief" (1 Nephi 12:22). There would be no comfort for the sorrowful, no forgiveness for the penitent, no peace for those blown to and fro by the wayward winds of the world. Certainly, none of us would invite such a circumstance, for life without the Holy Ghost would truly be no life at all. Yet, we often fail to act on the guidance he offers, as if he were simply an optional part of our lives. We sometimes pay him so little attention when, actually, we need him so much. How long can we set aside his promptings, fail to act on his instruction, and not offend him? We would not buy a new car, put it in the garage, throw away the key, and never drive it; yet we pay a much higher price to receive the gift of the Holy Ghost and then quite often neglect to use that gift in a significant way. We would certainly understand the folly of a map never opened, a recipe never followed, a letter written but never sent. But do we understand what we forfeit when the Spirit's direction does not take root in our lives, when inspiration does not move us to action, when we do not respond as he patiently whispers over and over again? No one who is genuinely striving to live a righteous life would ever fail to act upon his words. No one who treasures the Spirit's whisperings would ever do anything except listen and then take action.

STEP NINE

The full effect of the Holy Ghost is only felt when we discipline ourselves to act upon the promptings we hear. By this point, you have increased your sensitivity to the Spirit and are now even more aware of his presence in your life. As wonderful as this is, however, it is not enough. As his inspiration pierces our hearts, we must respond to the guidance and instruction of the Holy Ghost. For the next five days, resolve to act on any inspiration you receive from the Holy Ghost, despite the inconvenience or the consequences. Do not let anything delay or distract you from your goal. When you hear the Spirit whisper, stay focused on that prompting until you have done something about it. Record your experiences in your scripture journal.

From the scripture journal of Nephi:

> *If ye will enter in by the way, and receive the Holy Ghost, it will show unto you all things what ye should do.*
>
> —2 NEPHI 32:5

From the scripture journal of the apostle Paul:

> *Walk in the Spirit.*
>
> —GALATIANS 5:16

CHAPTER TEN

WE MUST WRITE HIS WORDS

*I command all men . . . that they shall write the
words which I speak unto them.*
2 NEPHI 29:11

The Holy Ghost is always speaking. Some promptings require one-time, immediate actions that once fulfilled can be forgotten. For example, we may feel inspired to visit a friend, to shovel a neighbor's snowy walk, or to forgive a debt. But often, the guidance we receive must be remembered longer because our response will be ongoing and long-term. This type of prompting requires sustained effort: to be more loving, to study a certain gospel subject, or to share the gospel with a friend. This inspiration must not be forgotten. We must record, remember, and review it as time goes by.

We certainly cannot live by the whisperings of the Spirit if we do not have a way to remember what he says. Recording our promptings is critical to retaining them, which is critical to recalling them, and we must certainly be able to recall them if we ever hope to live by them. Elder Richard G. Scott said, "Powerful spiritual direction in your life can be overcome or forced into the background unless you provide a way to retain it" ("Acquiring," 88). Not only should the whisperings of the Spirit be written, figuratively speaking, on our hearts, but they should be written down, literally, on paper as well.

This advice is not new; we have heard it many times before. Elder Sterling W. Sill reminded us of the Lord's instructions to one of his servants:

"In an interesting 'time-machine experience,' John the Apostle was permitted actually to preview the judgment. This revelation was of such great consequence that thereafter he has been called John the Revelator. However, this revelation was not given for John's benefit alone. The Lord specifically instructed him to write down what he saw so that we might see it also. John says that . . . he heard a voice behind him. It was a great voice as of a trumpet 'Saying, I am Alpha and Omega, the first and the last: and, What thou seest, write in a book, . . . ' (Rev. 1:11.)" (Conference Report, Apr. 1964, 14).

A key point of this passage is that John, like other prophets before and after him, was the Lord's appointed mouthpiece to reveal to us what God would have us know. It was intended that each of us would, through John, share in his experience and, through the Holy Ghost, receive a witness of the truth contained therein.

What would have happened if he had failed to write down

his experience? What if he had lost his journal or was too tired and wanted to go to bed—excuses we often use ourselves? If not for John's diligent obedience, this magnificent vision would not have been preserved as we have it. If John had not recorded his vision, we would not know what John learned that day. We would be without his words or the eternal truths we learn from them. It would truly have been an incalculable loss.

Similarly, *we* are not given communication from the Spirit simply for our own benefit. Of course, we are given answers pertinent to our own lives, but others will be blessed, as well, through the inspiration and instruction we receive. The times our faith was strengthened, trials that deepened our relationship with God, moments of personal communion with the heavens—each experience we have with the Spirit, if recorded, will live much longer than we will and touch others' lives in ways we might otherwise be unable to.

Moses was instructed to "write the things which [the Lord] shall speak" (Moses 1:40). Elder Anthon H. Lund said, "From the days of Moses until the days of the Apostles, He gave revelations, and inspired His servants to write them. How thankful we are that these records have been kept! Moses has been called God's first pen." Elder Lund taught that recording inspiration helps us understand the never-changing nature of the Lord. He said, "The earliest authentic writings we have come from him, and, studying them, we see how consistent is the word of God from beginning to end" (Conference Report, Oct. 1901, 22).

When the prophet Jacob was given charge of the sacred record of his people, he was also commanded to write the important things "upon these plates" (Jacob 1:4). We are the beneficiaries of those individuals through the ages who responded to the Lord's direction and wrote down the things the Holy Ghost prompted them to record. Without their words—the scriptures—we, like the posterity of Lehi, would certainly be lost.

One evening I noticed my fifteen-year-old son studying for a history test. He caught my attention because he was writing on a small index card for a very long time. I finally asked him what he was doing. His history teacher allowed each student, for one test during the semester, to take with them into the test a small index card on which they had written as much information as humanly possible. My son wrote and rewrote his card, trying to discover new ways to squeeze a whole chapter into a very small space. It was a work of art when he finished! I remember thinking if he had only spent as much time studying as he did rearranging the words on that card, he would certainly have passed with flying colors. (But of course he would not have had nearly as much fun!) He did pass the test and later admitted that he would never have made it without the information he had written on that card. Apparently, his hours of work—well, let's call it art—paid off.

Through our mortal schooling we are all given tests. Fortunately for us, we are also given the answers. Our answers come from the Holy Ghost—our heavenly tutor—and we, too, can write them down. Unlike my son the history student, we have unlimited writing space. Unlike Nephi, who had to be cautious about the space he used, we are not restricted in how much we can write, nor do we have the time-consuming task of engraving on metal plates. We are free to record every communication we receive from the Holy Ghost and can do so with very little trouble or inconvenience. There is always a reason he speaks when he does, and recording our personal promptings will help us realize just what those reasons are. With his help, we can more easily pass through mortality. With him by our side, mortality can be an open-book test. If we will live by his direction, we will not fail.

President James E. Faust said, "We are bombarded on all sides by a vast number of messages we don't want or need. More information is generated in a single day than we can absorb in a lifetime" ("Standing," 62). Truly, we live in an age when an incredible amount of data is exchanged every single minute. The amount directed specifically toward us is more than we can possibly process or comprehend. We can never hope to remember it all. It is the same with the communications of the Holy Ghost. Through him, we are given incredible amounts of spiritual information; we call them spiritual promptings. These promptings come often. So often, in fact, that the more proficient we become at hearing them, the more we recognize just how many times he truly does speak. Because of the tremendous amount and importance of the spiritual communication given us, relying solely on our memory to retain it all would strain the limitations of a mortal mind. Without some way to remember what we are taught, we will forget these very personal, heavenly promptings. At the very least, the details will dim; we could even lose them forever. Either way, if a record of those promptings is not preserved, what we have been given will eventually diminish and we will live without inspiration meant especially for us. The loss of such communication from our Father in Heaven is immeasurable when we consider how vital it is to our progression and eventual perfection.

Once we decide to write down the Spirit's promptings, we will be surprised at how many times he speaks. In actuality, he is speaking as much as ever; it is our listening ear that has suddenly become more aware. Because there is so much, we may ask, Which things should we record? As our spirits become more sensitive to the presence of the Holy Ghost, we will learn to know more easily which things are most important to preserve.

And then we must begin. For such recording to be a truly significant experience, we must be motivated by the desire to remember our promptings from the Spirit, not simply to fulfill a requirement or fill space in a journal. If we write out of duty alone, most likely it will not be a meaningful or satisfying experience, and we will tire of the exercise quickly.

Instead, we must fill our journals with those things that reflect our spirit—our thoughts, desires, interests, goals, and dreams. Whenever something makes us stop and think, we must write it down. Whenever we hear something that brings the thought to our mind, "*That is really good*," the Spirit is prompt-ing us to record what we heard. It may be a quotation from a Relief Society lesson or a thought that comes at a fireside or while we are driving to work or folding laundry. It may be a motto we want to adopt or a goal we feel inspired to work toward. Whenever we feel our spirit nudged, that is an indica-tion the Holy Ghost is present. We must write down things we feel, think, believe, desire, understand, decide, learn, or know at that very moment, for what we hear with our spiritual ears is instruction directly from God, declared by the soft and still voice we know as the Holy Ghost. The Spirit's whisperings are never insignificant; they are always given to fulfill the Lord's purposes. It is up to us to record the moments he speaks so we can more fully understand his will in our lives.

Sometimes the actual words spoken are not the most impor-tant thing to remember, for the words may simply be the cata-lyst that awakens our spiritual understanding. Usually, it is what we *feel* that is the real treasure. For example, we do not neces-sarily need to record every word spoken in a talk in sacrament meeting. It is not the words as much as it is the feelings they evoke within us that have the power to change us. We recognize that "the actual words of the talks are the same for everyone, but the spiritual insights and the promptings and proddings of the Spirit will not be the same for all. Therefore the most impor-tant notes to record in our journals would be those personal 'flashes' of insight and inspiration—when we learn some-thing new, when something that has personal relevance and application is spoken to the mind and heart, or when the Spirit prompts us to make changes in our life. As we listen to the [general conference] speakers we can, as Nephi said of the scriptures, liken their words to ourselves, our unique circumstances, the needs and desires of our hearts. In this manner general conference is transformed from institutional instruction to inspiration of individuals" (Top, et al., *Follow,* 138).

What is spoken to our minds and to our hearts contains the most value for us, for those are the very personal communications given us by the Holy Ghost. What we should remember—and record—are these unique impressions, their individual meaning, and the distinctive inspiration that comes to us alone. These principles can be applied to all gospel learning. Attempting to write down an entire fireside talk would not be nearly as meaningful as writing down the personal inspiration we received concerning our own life as we were listening to the talk. It is at these moments—moments when we hear the voice of the Spirit speak to us individually—that we are able to feel the Lord's love as well as his personal interest in our lives.

President Boyd K. Packer said:

"Inspiration comes more easily in peaceful settings. Such words as *quiet, still, peaceable, Comforter* abound in the scriptures. . . .

"The world grows increasingly noisy" ("Reverence," 21–22).

The Spirit's voice is best heard in the quiet moments of our day. Most of us can't imagine the words *quiet* and *our day* being in the same sentence, let alone being a realistic goal. But if you watch closely, you will find moments here and there to spend with the Holy Ghost, listening. Set your morning alarm ten minutes earlier than usual; by lunchtime you will barely remember you sacrificed that time. Take advantage of children's naptimes, your workplace lunch hour, driving alone in the car, or the time you spend in the shower.

Once you discover quiet time, invite the Spirit through prayer and give him every opportunity to speak. Because most days are driven by schedules, we can set aside blocks of time for the things that encourage communication from the Holy Ghost. Scheduling time for scripture study, pondering, and even just sitting alone in the quiet will settle our spirits and strengthen our ability to live according to the inspiration we receive. Noise of any kind will easily overpower even the loudest whispering of the Spirit and keep us from hearing those things intended especially for us.

Just for fun, I sent my brother an e-mail at the end of a typical day listing the things I had done in that eighteen-hour period: the carpools, the errands, the shopping, the laundry, the meals, the ballgames, the homework, the phone calls, the cleaning, and the dishes. I actually forgot to mention the broken hearts mended, the pep talks given, the lessons taught, and the never-ending list of tugs on my emotional resources. He said it made him tired just reading it! The problem is, that was not just an isolated day. *Every* day is like that day—not just for me, but for all of us. Mary Engelbreit said it perfectly: "Life is just so *daily!*" (2008 calendar).

There is no way around it. We all live very busy—and very noisy—lives. If it is a battle we are fighting for peace and quiet in our day, certainly the first casualty is our ability to hear and remember inspiration spoken by the Holy Ghost. And when we do hear his whisperings, we place ourselves in a difficult position if we expect to recall these experiences despite the unpredictable chaos of our everyday lives. "Even a touching, spiritual moment," reminded Elder Neal A. Maxwell, "can be so quickly lost in the bustle of an afternoon's traffic jam, in the cares of tonight's phone calls, or because of the pressures brought by tomorrow's mail" (*Rejoice,* 112).

Writing things down as we are prompted by the Spirit makes the difference in whether we will remember them or simply let them slip away amidst the busyness of everyday life. Writing down the promptings we receive increases the likelihood that the Spirit will speak to us again. Elder Neal A. Maxwell taught this principle when he said: "The prompting that goes unresponded to may not be repeated. Writing down what we have been prompted with is vital. A special thought can also be lost later in the day in the rough and tumble of life. God should not, and may not, choose to repeat the prompting if we assign what was given such a low priority as to put it aside" (*Quote,* 171).

Recording the glimpses of knowledge and truth given us by the Spirit isn't just a good idea—it is a necessity. At the moment they are received, we cannot imagine ever forgetting them. But even the sharpest memory is limited in what it can retain and for how long. We cannot fill our bucket with spiritual knowledge and forget to plug the leak! We must find a way to keep all that the Spirit offers us. If we do not, we are consciously choosing to walk alone. Communing with the heavens is no small thing; we trivialize the process when we fail to remember what they say.

During the years my husband presided over the Massachusetts Boston Mission, we spoke often to the missionaries. There was no greater feeling than to look down from the pulpit and into the eyes of a missionary who was eagerly focused on what we were saying. What was even more touching was to see him pull out a pen and piece of paper and hurriedly write down something we had said. When we saw that, we knew something wonderful had happened: The Spirit had touched his heart. We taught our missionaries to take notes as the Spirit spoke to them. Doing so would show the Lord, as it showed us, that they valued something they heard and treasured something they felt.

Elder Gene R. Cook teaches of another blessing that comes as we record sacred experiences. His family had recorded memorable spiritual events in order to remember them. "Many of the stories . . . were just small, everyday experiences. But because we wrote them down, thought about them, and discussed them, they *became* spiritual experiences. Part of the key to having spiritual experiences is simply to recognize them, value them, and treat them with enough respect to record them. Surely the Lord taught us well through the Prophet Joseph Smith, who, after his great vision of the heavenly kingdoms, said, 'This is the end of the vision which we saw, which we were commanded to write while we were yet in the Spirit' (D&C 76:113)" (*Raising*, 171).

The scriptures tell us that Adam and Eve kept a "book of remembrance" (Moses 6:5) so spiritual truths taught them would not be forgotten. An added benefit of such a record is the gratitude and humility that come as we continually reflect on the goodness of the Lord. President Spencer W. Kimball said, "Those who keep a book of remembrance are more likely to keep the Lord in remembrance in their daily lives" (*Teachings*, 349). As we remember and record and review the communications of the Spirit, our lives are blessed in numerous ways, including the following:

1. The Spirit's promptings turn into ideas, which turn into goals. They become stars to steer by, inspiring spiritual growth.

2. The promptings builds testimony twice: once when the inspiration comes and again when we reflect on it later. Sometimes inspiration is given for today. But often it is given for us to draw upon in the future. Writing it down ensures that we will have it when we need it.

3. The inspiration makes our scripture study especially productive because writing down inspiration that comes as we study causes us to evaluate more closely the things we read. The process of putting feelings into words requires us to contemplate more deeply and define more exactly what each word means to us personally.

4. We are reminded of the way the Holy Ghost works in our lives, giving us hope during difficult times and confidence that he will be there again to lead us through the darkness, when it comes.

5. Our record helps us recall quotations and scriptures that have made a difference to us and which may make a difference to others, as we share them in talks, in lessons, or simply in conversation with a friend down the street who is struggling with a particular problem.

6. We have a systematic way of keeping notes on teaching topics, including essential information that helps us more efficiently teach that particular principle.

7. We are reminded of our blessings. Counting them makes challenges easier to bear and joys even sweeter.

8. As we read back over the things we record, the Holy Ghost continues to testify to us of their truthfulness, helping us learn and relearn the spiritual truths we have been taught.

Consider again the worthy servants of God who recognized the Holy Ghost and, upon hearing his voice, acted upon his inspiration. We, too, hear his voice; we, too, must respond. Recording his promptings keeps them always in our minds; living true to them keeps them always in our hearts.

Before the destroying angel passed over Egypt, the Israelites were instructed to mark their doors with lamb's blood to identify themselves to the Lord and thus escape his judgment. We, too, can show the Lord we are his by recording the promptings of the Spirit—his words given directly to us.

When the Savior, after his resurrection, appeared to the Nephites, he inquired about "other scriptures" he had commanded them to write concerning the fulfillment of the prophecies of Samuel the Lamanite (3 Nephi 23:6). The Lord asked his disciples, "How be it that ye have not written this thing . . . ?" He again "commanded that it should be written; therefore it was written according as he commanded" (3 Nephi 23:11, 13).

Imagine the feelings of the prophet Nephi when he was asked by the Savior himself why the record had been neglected, why certain things had not been written down. The scriptures do not mention the sorrow Nephi must have felt in his heart or his determination never to neglect this sacred writing again. We can only guess his feelings on the matter for the account simply states, "Nephi remembered that this thing had not been written" (3 Nephi 23:12). Certainly he felt deep regret for failing to do as the Lord had commanded.

The Lord speaks to us through Nephi, the son of Lehi: "I command all men, . . . that they shall write the words which I speak unto them" (2 Nephi 29:11). We, too, have been commanded to record the words of the Lord in our lives. These words, brought by the Holy Ghost, are sacred, and we are the appointed record-keepers. We cannot neglect *our* sacred record. Recording the whisperings of the Spirit is more than a good idea; it is a commandment given by God, and when the Lord speaks, covenant people listen—and obey.

STEP TEN

Prepare your scripture journal to hold in its pages your experiences with the Holy Ghost. Because this is your own record, you can organize it however you would like and according to your own needs. There is no right or wrong way! Whatever works best for you is exactly the way you should do it.

Consider dividing your journal into sections. The length of each will be determined by how much you hope to write on that particular topic. Title each with a specific topic. Choose from the topics below, or come up with your own. (Hint: Think of what you would like most to leave behind for your posterity and choose those topics first.)

Favorite Quotations   Favorite Scriptures
Letters to Children   Favorite Lines from Hymns
Goals   Insights into the Scriptures
Life Mottos   Gratitudes
Notes from Church Meetings

If you like to remember quotations, you might want to use a large section of your journal to record the quotations that touch your heart (that feeling is the Holy Ghost inspiring you!). If you would like, you can choose topics and evenly divide your pages, writing a different topic on the first page of each section. Or, you can simply write as you go and not worry about placing them in any particular order.

If you decide to choose specific topics, here are a few ideas as you begin:

Adversity

Book of Mormon

Charity

Commitment

Conversion

Education

Faith

Forgiveness

Friendship

Gratitude

Happiness

Home

Holy Ghost

Humility

Jesus Christ

Love

Missionary Work

Obedience

Prophets

Revelation

Righteousness

Service

Scriptures

Temple

Tithing

Wisdom

Work

CHAPTER ELEVEN

SCRIPTURE JOURNALS, A SACRED RECORD

Written not with ink, but with the Spirit of the living God.
2 CORINTHIANS 3:3

A lthough I have learned about the Holy Ghost my entire life, it has taken me nearly half a century of living to recognize the many times he speaks to me. As I have become more aware of his influence, I have become equally aware that I can respond to his promptings only as accurately as I can remember what he said.

Several years ago, I realized I needed to record things the Spirit told me. Many times as I felt his promptings, I would frantically search for something on which to write them down: sacrament meeting programs, the back of Sunday lesson materials, pieces of old envelopes, and the margins of books. I even found a few empty places in the back of my scriptures—so I wrote there, too. Before long, I had words and quotations and thoughts and ideas written everywhere I looked. When I needed to recall something that had touched me, I would wade through the loose papers that seemed to end up just about everywhere or thumb through my scriptures trying to decipher the scribbled notes in the back. Occasionally I found what I was looking for, but usually I ended up with nothing but frustration. It bothered me that I might be losing information the Lord wanted me to have. I knew these promptings were meant to help me and that I, in turn, was meant to remember them. Someday, I thought, I will need them and not know where to find them. How could I hold on to those pieces of spiritual information that had already come to me?

The attainment of any knowledge—temporal or spiritual—is always coupled with the responsibility to live true to it. One day, I read the following, which changed the way I viewed the lessons of the Spirit: "When we receive promptings from the Holy Ghost, it is like opening an imaginary door between the spirit mind and the mortal mind. When this happens, we receive knowledge which we cannot deny. . . . We will be held accountable for that knowledge in the day of judgment" (Eldred G. Smith, Conference Report, Apr. 1963, 18).

I remember reading over that passage several times just to be sure I had read it correctly. Could the Lord really hold us responsible for the little bursts of inspiration he sends us? Does it really matter what we do with the promptings we are given? The answer was obvious, and I felt like a child who had forgotten to study for a test: totally unprepared and slightly panicked!

I knew I needed to start writing—in some organized way—everything the Spirit was teaching me, for someday I might be asked if I had lived true to what I was given.

That very day, I bought a leather journal, added a few tabs and extra pages, glued in some topics and dividers, and began to keep a record of the whisperings of the Spirit in my life. I recorded every new insight, every prompting, and every quotation that touched me. I made a point of writing down each new understanding gained and every time the Spirit testified to me of truth. Whenever I had an "aha" moment, I wrote it down.

Ever since I began to write in this journal, I have more fully realized the incredible number of times the Spirit speaks to me. Every day I watch and wait for those moments: from sparks of inspiration to deep and abiding peace in my heart; from sudden understanding of a principle to pure knowledge that is unquestionable evidence of the Holy Ghost. These spiritual insights, personal promptings, and life lessons have become a permanent part of me as I have recorded them on paper as well as in my heart.

This journal has become, to me, a sacred record, a testament of the very personal and profound workings of the Spirit in my life. I call it my scripture journal, for its pages are filled with revelation—personal revelation. Simply put, our scriptures—the standard works—are *also* scripture journals; they, too, are filled with revelation. Elder Theodore M. Burton taught, "As a people we ought to write of our own lives and our own experiences to form a sacred record for our descendants. We must provide for them the same uplifting, faith-promoting strength that the ancient scriptures now give us" ("Inspiration," 17).

Much like Nephi or Moroni or Moses, I have borne testimony in my scripture journal to those who come after me through the words I have chosen to leave behind. My hope is that this book will be a treasure of truth for my posterity.

As time has passed, I have found more reasons to begin more journals, and now my husband tells me that I "lead the league in journals." I admitted once that I am not a very good journal-keeper, and when the women sitting near me heard that, they laughed. (I had three journals on my lap!) I do have a difficult time writing down lists of what I have done during a day, in the hope that sometime in the future some distant relative may be entertained by it. But to create scripture journals—meaningful records of the influences of the Holy Ghost in my life—well, that is quite a different story.

Scripture journals allow others to understand your mind and take a look inside your heart. As Nephi wrote upon the plates, for instance, he identified how he chose what to include in the record: "Upon these I write the things of my soul" (2 Nephi 4:15). When we read the writings of Nephi, we get a glimpse inside his mind and heart, for we know from this scripture that these are the things he held dear. Similarly, the prophet Jacob recorded things of a sacred nature to strengthen his people. He said, "And if there were preaching which was sacred, or revelation which was great, or prophesying, that I should engraven the heads of them upon these plates, and touch upon them as much as it were possible, for Christ's sake, and for the sake of our people" (Jacob 1:4). We, too, are strengthened as we read the words of the prophets—those things which were especially meaningful to them.

President Spencer W. Kimball will always be remembered for his constant encouragement to keep journals. He said, "I promise you that if you will keep your journals and records they will indeed be a source of great inspiration to your families, to your children, your grandchildren, and others, on through the generations" ("Hold," 4). He also said, "Journals are a way of counting our blessings and leaving an inventory of these blessings for our posterity" (*Teachings,* 349). No matter how old we are, how many experiences we have already had with the Holy Ghost, or how well we do or do not write, we cannot delay another moment. We must begin now, for every word we record will bless our lives and the lives of those we love.

My maternal grandfather died before I was born. As a child, I saw pictures of him in our family Book of Remembrance. Other than that, I knew little about him. That all changed, though, the day I found a packet of letters in my mother's belongings. They were letters to her from her father, written the year she left home for college. As I read them and reflected on the feelings and emotions revealed there, my grandfather came alive for me. I began to create in my mind a picture of this wonderful man I had never met. My love for him deepened as the Spirit spoke to me of his goodness. I wish I had known him in mortality. And although that great blessing was denied me, I have no doubt I will someday meet him on the other side. I will meet him and I will know him, not from a photograph but from reading his tender words to a daughter he loved so much.

Isn't that precisely what the scriptures are in our lives—letters from a Heavenly Father to his children, inviting us to know him? Aren't they filled with words of counsel and love to guide us, messages that open our eyes and provide insight into who he is and the eternal nature of our relationship to him? As we read his words, our love for him deepens, and we truly come to *know* him.

When I die, I am just selfish enough to not want to be forgotten! I want my children's children's children to know that I was more than just a name on a pedigree chart—that I was really here. As they read my scripture journal, it is my hope that they will come to *know me*. I hope they will understand, because I recorded them, what the promptings of the Spirit meant to me. And because of that insight, I pray they will also be inspired to seek the Spirit and live by his whisperings in their lives.

Elder Orson Pratt once said: "If every Elder had . . . kept a faithful record of all that he had seen, heard, and felt of the goodness, wisdom, and power of God, the Church would now have been in the possession of many thousand volumes, containing much important and useful information. How many thousands have been miraculously healed in this Church, and yet no one has recorded the circumstances. Is this right? Should these miraculous manifestations of the power of God be forgotten and pass into oblivion? Should the knowledge of these things slumber in the hearts of those who witnessed them, and extend no farther than their own verbal reports will carry them? This negligence on the part of the servants of God ought no longer to exist. We should keep a record because Jesus has commanded it. We should keep a record because the same will benefit us and the generations of our children after us" (*Star*, 152).

Our own written words may be instrumental in bringing our posterity to Christ. Knowing that, is there one of us who would not perform such a labor of love, for that reason alone? We can echo the words of Nephi: "For we labor diligently to write, to persuade our children, and also our brethren, to believe in Christ, and to be reconciled to God" (2 Nephi 25:23). As we record our experiences with the Holy Ghost and create our own scripture journal, we can bless the lives of those who come after us. We will show our posterity who we really were. In this way, we invite them to know us—and remember us.

Before the missionaries left Boston to return home from our mission, we asked them to write their responses to a series of questions about their mission experience as well as their most cherished memories. The first page began, "I, Elder Smith, having been born of goodly parents . . ." It was to become the beginning of their personal scripture record, to be passed on to the generations that followed. We hoped they would continue to add to it, read it occasionally, and treasure it. It contained the feelings of their hearts.

Lord Byron once said:

Words and things, and a small drop of ink,
Falling like dew, upon a thought, produces
That which makes thousands, perhaps millions, think.
                                        (QuoteWorld.org)

We have the chance to leave for others an account of our heavenly tutoring—our experiences with the Holy Ghost in mortality. Through these words, we can contribute to the lives of those who come after us by causing them to think about the importance of the Spirit's whisperings in their own lives. What could we give them that would be of more worth?

STEP ELEVEN

Write another letter to your posterity, this one on the very last page of your scripture journal. Include your testimony of the importance of the Holy Ghost and remind them that this is a gift available to all of God's children. Remind them to live worthy of the Spirit, to listen for his whisperings, to record his inspiration, and to live by his every word.

Take your scripture journal with you to your church meetings. Lay it open next to you as you study the scriptures at home. Keep it always nearby so you can easily record the moments you feel inspired by something you hear or are moved by the feelings of your heart. These things, and others you will discover along the way, are evidence of the Holy Ghost.

You are now on your way. Strive to walk daily with the Holy Ghost. You will be led by him in ways that at one time you might not have recognized. Now that you have become more familiar with his voice and more committed to following his guidance, you will receive all that the Holy Ghost has to offer. You will live a life directed by the Spirit. You will feel spiritual growth as never before. You will be led by God, not man. And you, too, will be led by the whisperings of the Spirit.

From the scripture journal of Joseph Smith:

> *I will impart unto you of my Spirit, which shall enlighten your mind, which shall fill your soul with joy.*
>
> —DOCTRINE AND COVENANTS 11:13

CHAPTER TWELVE

"GOD'S FINEST WHISPERS"

I will pour out my spirit unto you,
I will make known my words unto you.
PROVERBS 1:23

S ome years ago, a story in the newspaper told of a young
woman with Down's syndrome who was unable to speak
well enough to be understood. She had learned instead
to communicate through a computer that spoke aloud each
word she typed on her keyboard. Up until that time, her world
had been silent, every thought and feeling locked inside by the
physical restrictions of her mortal body. Now, for the first time
in her life, she had a voice. It was as if she had been set free.
Hour after hour, she practiced typing, and as she did, her world
opened up before her eyes. Those around her were amazed
at what they heard and saw. She wrote about things no one
supposed she even had the capacity to notice, let alone

comprehend. She began to write poetry and through the beauty of her words expressed the deepest feelings of her heart.

One day her mother discovered a printed sheet of paper on the table near her daughter's computer. The words her daughter had written were sensitive, insightful, and moving. One line, in particular, caught her mother's eye. It was short, yet it spoke volumes. Not only did it bear testimony of her daughter's unique connection to God but it also beautifully illustrated what is possible for each of us as we open our spiritual ears and listen to the soft and gentle voice of the Holy Ghost. The words were simple and few, but the meaning they carried was transforming. She wrote: "I hear God's finest whispers."

Through the influence of the Spirit, we, too, can begin to comprehend things that we previously had barely noticed. We can rise above the restrictions of our mortal bodies and understand spiritual truths as never before. We, too, can hear God's finest whispers.

Throughout time, mankind has been fascinated by the possibility of communicating through the veil. When I was eight years old, my young, newly married aunt died suddenly and unexpectedly. I knew by the reactions of my grandparents and family members that it was a terrible tragedy, but with the logic of a little child, I was puzzled by their longing for her in the weeks and months following. I wanted to suggest they do what I did: pray to Heavenly Father and, in a way reminiscent of a telephone conversation, just ask him if they could talk to her. I spent many extra minutes on my knees those days, talking to

Aunt Margaret as if she had only gone on a long vacation. I never doubted she could hear me, and I felt happy to know she was not far away.

The memory of my eight-year-old, oversimplified view of communicating with the spirit world always brings a smile to my face. But I always feel great comfort in knowing that the veil truly is thin, that communication between both sides, in both directions, is not only possible but certain.

The Lord, in his generosity, bestowed upon us the magnificent gift of the Holy Ghost. As always, our welfare is his greatest concern. His love for us continues to rescue us from danger and shield us from impending doom. If it were not for his goodness, we would be unable to overcome the powers that work against us in mortality.

A veil of forgetfulness separates us from the life we once knew and that to which we will return someday. For now, we are given the privilege of walking not by the audible sound of the Lord's voice but by the soft whisperings of the Holy Ghost. He is our gift for as long as we need him, our friend through any circumstance that may arise. He will never leave us unless we offend him, never desert us unless we drive him away. He must certainly love us, for his entire purpose is to guide, direct, and return us to the presence of God. Those who live by his whispers will, indeed, receive magnificent blessings, for in the words of Elder Bruce R. McConkie: "The gift of the Holy Ghost is the greatest of all the gifts of God, as pertaining to this life; and those who enjoy that gift here and now, *will inherit eternal life hereafter,* which is the greatest of all the gifts of God in eternity" (*Messiah,* 2:122; emphasis added).

Relatively speaking, the day is not far off when the mission of the Holy Ghost on our behalf will be complete and we will return home. Our mortal journey will end, and we will stand in the presence of the Lord. He will draw us close, and we will speak with him, finally—face to face. At that moment, we will hear his voice and remember we have heard it before. It will be a joyous day and a sweet and wonderful reunion.

Certainly at that sacred time, we will also come to know more fully another member of the Godhead, the constant and loyal friend who has walked with us through all our years in mortality: the Holy Ghost. We will certainly recognize his familiar voice, for we will have heard his whispers and felt his influence throughout the time of our earthly experience. Perhaps we will, at that day, find adequate words to thank him for his tender and watchful care.

For now, we can express our gratitude as we learn to listen and strive to live by his gentle guidance; we can seek his presence and live worthy of all he has to offer us. Most important, we can gratefully acknowledge his divine role in our lives and learn to live by the light he bestows.

An incredible moment in Church history came when Oliver Cowdery, reflecting on the experience of translating the Book of Mormon, exclaimed, "These were days never to be forgotten!" I echo his words and stand in awe as I consider the times in which we live, knowing the heavens are still open, that truth descends on and illuminates our souls like dew on the trees in the fresh morning sunlight. Heavenly manifestations have not ceased. Just as miraculously as in days past, we can hear the voice of the Lord. Through the Holy Ghost, he speaks to us. May we receive his words, record them, remember them, and always live by what we are given.

From the scripture journal of the Prophet Joseph Smith:

> *Great things shall be accomplished by you from this hour; and you shall begin to feel the whisperings of the Spirit of God; . . . and you shall be endowed with power from on high.*
>
> —JOSEPH SMITH (*HISTORY,* 2:182)

Sources

Alldredge, Ida R. *Improvement Era,* Dec. 1923, 114.

Ashton, Marvin J. *Be of Good Cheer.* Salt Lake City: Deseret Book, 1987.

———. "The Measure of Our Hearts." *Ensign,* Nov. 1988, 15.

Ballard, M. Russell. "Pure Testimony." *Ensign,* Nov. 2004, 40.

———. *Our Search for Happiness: An Invitation to Understand The Church of Jesus Christ of Latter-day Saints.* Salt Lake City: Deseret Book, 1993.

Bartlett, John. *Familiar Quotations.* Ed. Christopher Morley. 12th ed. Boston: Little, Brown, 1948.

Benson, Ezra Taft. *Come unto Christ.* Salt Lake City: Deseret Book, 1983.

———. *The Teachings of Ezra Taft Benson.* Salt Lake City: Bookcraft, 1988.

Best-Loved Poems of the LDS People. Ed. Jack M. Lyon, Linda Ririe Gundry, Jay A. Parry, and Devan Jensen. Salt Lake City: Deseret Book, 1996.

Burton, Theodore M. "The Inspiration of a Family Record." *Ensign,* Jan. 1977, 13.

Byron, George Gordon, Lord. "Words and Things." QuoteWorld.org. Accessed Jan. 2008.

Callis, Charles A. Conference Report, Apr. 1938, 98.

Cannon, George Q. *Gospel Truth.* Comp. Jerreld L. Newquist. 2d ed. 2 vols. Salt Lake City: Deseret Book, 1974.

Children's Songbook of The Church of Jesus Christ of Latter-day Saints. Salt Lake City: The Church of Jesus Christ of Latter-day Saints, 1989.

Cook, Gene R. *Living by the Power of Faith.* Salt Lake City: Deseret Book, 1985.

———. *Raising Up a Family to the Lord.* Salt Lake City: Deseret Book, 1993.

Engelbreit, Mary. "Mary Engelbreit's Life Is Just So Daily 2008 Family Calendar." Kansas City, Mo.: Andrews McMeel, 2007.

Ethnologue: Languages of the World. Ed. Raymond G. Gordon Jr. 15th ed. Dallas, Texas: SIL International, 2005.

Eyring, Henry B. "Write upon My Heart." *Ensign,* Nov. 2000, 85.

Faust, James E. "Born Again." *Ensign,* May 2001, 54.

———. "The Gift of the Holy Ghost." *Ensign,* May 1989, 31.

———. "Standing in Holy Places." *Ensign,* May 2005, 62.

Fedor, James H. "*Whisperings:* A Light Painting by Utah Lettering Artist James H. Fedor." Bountiful, Utah.

Grant, Heber J. *Gospel Standards.* Comp. G. Homer Durham. Salt Lake City: Improvement Era, 1941.

Hale, Heber Q. Conference Report, Apr. 1917, 106.

Hales, Robert D. "Receiving a Testimony of the Restored Gospel of Jesus Christ." *Ensign,* Nov. 2003, 28.

Hinckley, Gordon B. "God Is at the Helm." *Ensign,* May 1994, 53.

Hymns of The Church of Jesus Christ of Latter-day Saints. Salt Lake City: The Church of Jesus Christ of Latter-day Saints, 1985.

Journal of Discourses. 26 vols. London: Latter-day Saints' Book Depot, 1854–86.

Kendrick, L. Lionel. "Personal Revelation." In *Brigham Young University 1996–97 Speeches,* 251. Provo, Utah: Brigham Young University, 1997.

Kimball, Spencer W. Conference Report, Munich Germany Area Conference 1973, 74.

———. "Hold Fast to the Iron Rod." *Ensign,* Nov. 1978, 4.

———. "Revelation: The Word of the Lord to His Prophets." *Ensign,* May 1977, 76.

———. *The Teachings of Spencer W. Kimball.* Ed. Edward L. Kimball. Salt Lake City: Bookcraft, 1982.

Lee, Harold B. Conference Report, Apr. 1970, 54.

———. *The Teachings of Harold B. Lee.* Salt Lake City: Bookcraft, 1996.

Lewis, C. S. *Mere Christianity.* San Francisco: HarperCollins, 2001.

———. *The Problem of Pain.* San Francisco: HarperCollins, 2001.

Lund, Anthon H. Conference Report, Oct. 1901, 21.

Lund, Gerald N. *Selected Writings of Gerald N. Lund.* Gospel Scholars Series. Salt Lake City: Deseret Book, 1999.

Matthews, Robert J. *Selected Writings of Robert J. Matthews.* Gospel Scholars Series. Salt Lake City: Deseret Book, 1999.

Maxwell, Neal A. *The Neal A. Maxwell Quote Book.* Ed. Cory H. Maxwell. Salt Lake City: Bookcraft, 1997.

———. *"Not My Will, but Thine."* Salt Lake City: Bookcraft, 1988.

———. *Notwithstanding My Weakness.* Salt Lake City: Deseret Book, 1981.

———. *That My Family Should Partake.* Salt Lake City: Deseret Book, 1974.

———. *We Talk of Christ, We Rejoice in Christ.* Salt Lake City: Deseret Book, 1984.

———. *Wherefore, Ye Must Press Forward.* Salt Lake City: Deseret Book, 1977.

McConkie, Bruce R. *Mormon Doctrine.* 2d ed. Salt Lake City: Bookcraft, 1979.

———. *The Mortal Messiah: From Bethlehem to Calvary.* 4 vols. Salt Lake City: Deseret Book, 1979–81.

———. *A New Witness for the Articles of Faith.* Salt Lake City: Deseret Book, 1985.

McConkie, Joseph Fielding. *Gospel Symbolism.* Salt Lake City: Bookcraft, 1985.

Millet, Robert L. *Selected Writings of Robert L. Millet.* Gospel Scholars Series. Salt Lake City: Deseret Book, 2000.

Monson, Thomas S. *Inspiring Experiences That Build Faith.* Salt Lake City: Deseret Book, 1994.

———. "Sailing Safely the Seas of Life." *Ensign,* July 1999, 2.

Montgomery, Lucy Maud. *Anne of Green Gables.* New York: Avenel Books, 1985. Quoted in Maxwell, *"Not My Will,"* 9–10.

Oaks, Dallin H. "Always Have His Spirit." *Ensign,* Nov. 1996, 59.

———. "Teaching and Learning by the Spirit." *Ensign,* Mar. 1997, 6.

———. "Revelation." In *Classic Speeches: Twenty-Two Selections from Brigham Young University Devotional and Fireside Speeches.* Provo, Utah: Brigham Young University, 1994.

Packer, Boyd K. "The Candle of the Lord." *Ensign,* Jan. 1983, 51.

———. "Personal Revelation: The Gift, the Test, and the Promise." *Ensign,* Nov. 1994, 59.

———. "Prayers and Answers." *Ensign,* Nov. 1979, 19.

———. "Reverence Invites Revelation." *Ensign,* Nov. 1991, 21.

———. "A Sure Way to Happiness." *Church News,* 11 April 1998.

———. *"That All May Be Edified": Talks, Sermons and Commentary by Boyd K. Packer.* Salt Lake City: Bookcraft, 1982.

Paramore, James M. "The Gospel of Jesus Christ and Basic Needs of People." *Ensign,* May 1983, 27.

Perry, Janice Kapp. "A Child's Prayer." In *Children's Songbook of The*

Church of Jesus Christ of Latter-day Saints. Salt Lake City: The Church of Jesus Christ of Latter-day Saints, 1989.

Petersen, Mark E. *The Great Prologue.* Salt Lake City: Deseret Book, 1975.

Pratt, Orson. "Editorial." *Millennial Star* 11 (15 May 1849): 151.

———. *The Holy Spirit.* Quoted in Millet, *Writings,* 519–20.

Pratt, Parley P. *Key to the Science of Theology.* Salt Lake City: Deseret Book, 1965.

Roberts, B. H. *Man's Relationship to Deity.* Salt Lake City: Deseret News Press, 1901. Quoted in Millet, *Writings,* 204.

Romney, Marion G. Conference Report, Oct. 1961, 57.

Saint-Exupéry, Antoine de. *The Little Prince.* Trans. Katherine Woods. New York: Harcourt Brace Jovanovich, 1982.

Scott, Richard G. "Acquiring Spiritual Knowledge." *Ensign,* Nov. 1993, 86.

Sill, Sterling W. Conference Report, Apr. 1964, 11.

Smith, Eldred G. Conference Report, Apr. 1963, 18.

Smith, Joseph. *History of The Church of Jesus Christ of Latter-day Saints.* Ed. B. H. Roberts. 2d ed. rev. 7 vols. Salt Lake City: The Church of Jesus Christ of Latter-day Saints, 1932–51.

———. *Teachings of the Prophet Joseph Smith.* Sel. Joseph Fielding Smith. Salt Lake City: Deseret Book, 1938.

Smith, Joseph F. *Gospel Doctrine.* Salt Lake City: Deseret Book, 1939.

Smith, Joseph Fielding. *Answers to Gospel Questions.* Comp. Joseph Fielding Smith Jr. 5 vols. Salt Lake City: Deseret Book, 1957–66.

———. Conference Report, Apr. 1951, 59.

———. *Doctrines of Salvation.* Compiled by Bruce R. McConkie. 3 vols. Salt Lake City: Bookcraft, 1954–56.

Stapley, Delbert L. Conference Report, Oct. 1966, 111.

Talmage, James E. *The Articles of Faith.* Classics in Mormon Literature Edition. Salt Lake City: Deseret Book, 1984.

ThinkExist.com. Accessed Nov. 2007.

Top, Brent L., Larry E. Dahl, and Walter D. Bowen. *Follow the Living Prophets*. Salt Lake City: Bookcraft, 1993.

Wasserman, Jacob. *Columbus, Don Quixote of the Seas*. Trans. Eric Sutton (Boston: Little, Brown, 1930, 19–20). Quoted in Petersen, *Prologue*, 26.

Widtsoe, John A. *Man and the Dragon and Other Essays*. Salt Lake City: Bookcraft, 1945.

Woodruff, Wilford. *The Discourses of Wilford Woodruff*. Sel. G. Homer Durham. Salt Lake City: Bookcraft, 1946.

Young, Brigham. *Discourses of Brigham Young*. Sel. John A. Widtsoe. Salt Lake City: Deseret Book, 1941.

Young, Brigham, Jr. Conference Report, Apr. 1880, 31.

Young, S. Dilworth. Conference Report, Apr. 1953, 87.

INDEX

God, 35, 45, 46–47, 164; and
living church, 35–36; and
prophets, 35, 74, 115–16; and
priesthood, 35–36; living
without, 37–38, 84–86, 135;
appreciating, 39, 42, 100;
teaching children about, 39–41;
being worthy of, 41–42,
114–15; and prayer, 47, 49–50,
63–64, 104; gift of, 47, 164–65;
and obedience, 47–48, 110,
115; strengthens in trials,
51–52; voice of, 56–57, 76;
withdraws, 57, 110, 115; as
intermediary, 68, 73–74; and
responsibility, 83–84; gives
courage, 89; offending, 91;
strengthens relationships,
96–98; purifies, 98–99; and
decision making, 100; and
stewardship, 116–17. *See also*
Promptings
Horses, 33
Humility, 52, 96, 148

India, 53

Jacob, 140, 156–57
Jesus Christ: testimony of, 12;
Holy Ghost leads to, 14, 99;
baptism of, 18; relationship
with, 25, 94, 96; mission of, 30;
speaks through Holy Ghost,
73–74; missionaries teach of,
88–89; following, 89;
commands Nephites to write,
150
John, 24, 138–39
Journal, scripture: purpose for, 4–5;
and gratitude, 6; beginning, 7,
151–52; what to include in,
142–44; scheduling time to
keep, 145–46; organizing,
153–55; as sacred record, 155;
bless posterity, 155–60. *See also*
Record keeping
Joy, 11, 114

Kendrick, L. Lionel, 16, 75
Kimball, Spencer W.: on living
without revelation, 37; on still
small voice, 76; on record
keeping, 148, 157

Laban, 130–31
Laman, 12–13
Lamoni, 92
Languages, 71–73
Learning, 24
Lee, Harold B., 49–50
Lehi, 38
Lemuel, 12–13
Leprosy, 10–11
Letters, 157–58
Lewis, C. S., 77, 129–30
Light, 9